JOURNEY
of PRAISE

Josh Berletich
1039 Townline Rd 12
Willard, OH 44890

D1715330

JOURNEY
of PRAISE

Experiencing God's Blessings in
the Passing of our Mother

RANDY L. HORD

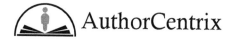 AuthorCentrix

Printed in the United States of America
ISBN 978-1-64133-378-8 (sc)
ISBN 978-1-64133-377-1 (e)

Library of Congress Control Number: 2018933069

Non-Fiction / Religion Spirituality and New Age / Biography / Autobiography
18.04.03

AuthorCentrix
25220 Hancock Ave #300,
Murrieta, CA 92562

www.authorcentrix.com

CONTENTS

DEDICATION

This book is dedicated to our Mother, Marilyn Hord without whose direction and undying love for her children and her Lord we would not have become the people we are today.

I also would like to dedicate it to her family especially her siblings and their families. They were also very instrumental in bringing this book to fruition. Their support of us during one of the darkest weeks of our lives was truly a blessing beyond description. My sister and her family were exceptional in keeping me focused on the real things that were important throughout our journey.

I also wish to dedicate this book to the fine staff of Toledo's St. Vincent's Medical Center. Their love, guidance and compassion during our stay there was incredible. They are an extraordinary group of people who love each patient as they would a member of their own family.

To my lovely wife, Cheryl and incredible daughter, Arielle. I love you both and I really appreciate your support in getting this book completed.

I would be greatly remiss if I didn't also mention my Lord and Savior. He is responsible for making me the man I am. He changed my life many years ago and I can only thank him daily for the person He has made me.

To you, the reader, this book is also dedicated. I hope you find encouragement, joy, and a closer walk with the Lord through reading it. May God bless you and may you have your own *Journey of Praise*.

CHAPTER 1

> *"...always giving thanks to God the Father for everything, in the name of our Lord Jesus Christ"*
>
> *– Ephesians 5:20 (NIV)*

"Hello, this is OnStar...we have received a signal that your mother's left air bag has been deployed in her garage."

This chilling statement was the second indication that something that wasn't good had happened to Mom. The first had come a moment earlier from my friend Don.

"Randy, this is Don. I just drove by your mother's house and there are two state highway patrol cars parked in the drive. Do you want me to go back and see what's going on and call you back?"

"No thanks", I said, "I'll go out and check." My wife, Cheryl, picked up the dinner she had prepared and put it in the microwave to wait until we returned. (We never got back to that dinner.) I was dressed in scrubby clothes from having just done chores at Mom's place. We had returned home less than an hour prior to the first call. We planned on a quiet night at home...little did we know what adventure God had planned for us.

We quickly hopped into our pickup truck and headed back to the farm. Almost immediately, my cell phone rang again. This time it was the local post of the Highway Patrol. "Is this Randy?"

"Yes Ma'am," I responded. After identifying herself, the dispatcher went on.

"We have officers at your mother's address, responding to an OnStar alert for a deployed driver-side air bag. They are looking for a way in to the house."

"I'm on my way, I'll be there in about 10 minutes with the key." I have to admit that I increased the speed limit a little bit and mentioned to Cheryl that this was not going to be good. But I still never really felt a sense of panic, only concern. Cheryl squeezed my hand in a comforting and loving way that only a wife of thirty-one years can do. In the seven days that followed, she showed that kind of love to everyone with whom she came into contact in a way that only a strong Christian wife can show. She was, and is, incredible.

When we arrived at the farm, a sheriff's car had joined the two cruisers from the OHSP. I unlocked the front door to find one of the officers already in the door to her garage with no car there.

"I'm Trooper (D). Do you have any idea where your mother is?"

"No Sir, I don't"

"We got the call, but there is no car here and we have no idea where the OnStar signal is coming from." More trepidation. "We had to break the window in the door to get entry to the house." His gentleness as we talked was comforting and I knew God's hand was on us.

"I'll try to call her on her cell phone."

Admittedly, by this point, my hands were shaking enough it was difficult to find her number in my contacts list. I dialed, no answer. I dialed again, no answer. I dialed a third time and a fourth and a fifth. On the sixth try, there was a click on the other end of the call. "Hello," a strong male voice answered.

"Who is this?" I inquired.

"Who is this?" the voice echoed.

"I'm Randy, I'm calling my mother's cell phone trying to reach her. Do I have the wrong number?"

"No, this is her cell phone, I'm Trooper P. Your mother's been in a crash. She's been life-flighted to Toledo St. Vincent's Medical Center."

I stumbled for words to say. "Oh, I see," was the only thing that would come out. "Where are you now?" I asked.

"I'm still at the scene. Are you able to come here and pick up her personal effects on your way to the hospital?" he asked. After describing to me where the crash occurred, and what they believed had caused it, we parted with his statement that he did not believe her injuries were life-threatening. That she was alert and talking to him at the scene and continued to do so with paramedics in the life flight chopper. For these reasons, he had made those statements. We would find out later that the injuries were much worse than any of them could have imagined. Cheryl and I headed to the crash scene to pick up whatever was there on the way to the hospital. We had fully an hour and a half drive to a place neither of us had ever been before and our Garmin was in our other vehicle.

As we drove to the scene, the words of Ephesians 5:20 came to me. To paraphrase: "in all things, give thanks." Why that verse came to me, I'm not really sure. I believe that in times of need, the Holy Spirit, the Great Comforter, comes to us and give us exactly and only what we need. Not a lot of extra stuff to cloud our minds, not so little we remain scared and nervous, but exactly what we need at that moment. The Holy Spirit gave me this verse. I felt compelled to respond. As I drove, it was a simple prayer I offered up to my Jesus and his Holy Father, but it made all the difference in the world. *"God, I don't understand why this has happened, but I thank you for it and ask for your guidance through it."* That twenty-one word prayer would prove to be more powerful, and, perhaps more significant, than any other prayer ten times as long that I had ever prayed. The following pages describe the incredible journey our family took and the multitude of blessings that God granted us in that journey. We were blessed. We were drawn closer to Him. But best of all, we praised His name and were constantly surrounded by other believers of all denominations. None caring what religious affiliation the other had, nor how their Sunday (or Saturday) church services were conducted. They all love Him, and they all loved us, and Mom. That, my friends, was truly the ultimate blessing that God gave us, and our Mother. We were about to set out on our *Journey of Praise.* Our leader? Jesus Christ. All we had to do was focus on Him, follow His leading and we were in for quite a ride.

CHAPTER 2

"God is our refuge and strength, an ever-present help in trouble. Therefore we will not fear…"

– Psalm 46:1 (NIV)

The crash scene was devastating! They had just finished loading the Chevrolet Silverado that the other driver had so recently been driving with four of his five kids. He, and the four young children in his dual cab pickup were on their way to the local hospital in one direction, while Mom's friend Alice was headed to the trauma unit at another more major hospital in the opposite direction. Alice would ultimately take a ground trip to another of Toledo's excellent hospitals for some surgery on her hand then, a few days later, she'd go home with her daughter. She's still dealing with the psychological effects of having been with her best friend in the horrific crash and not being able to do anything to help. Her story is one full of blessings as her part of this unbelievable journey.

Immediately following the crash, Alice told me later, there was a guardian angel who came and gently helped her out of the car and clear of the wreck. "He was", she said, "an incredibly gentle and loving man." He sat with her until the EMT's arrived and, having been an eyewitness to the crash became an excellent source of information for the investigating officer. Among our many blessings was that later, he and his wife sent us a card telling us who they were and expressing the most genuine and loving condolences. We were again given the most incredible gift any one could ask for…the love of other Christians through their expression of His grace. I served as an athletic director for a local high school, and less than a year after the crash, God brought this man across my path as a basketball official. Our League Commissioner had hired Lee over a year before the crash. WOW! God's plan is good.

As we walked past the tow truck on which the pickup was loaded, we could see Mom's Silver Malibu sitting sprawled across the ditch like a bridge, facing the road. Honestly, I have no clue how she possibly even survived the tangled and twisted mess. The jaws-of-life had done their work. The top was cut off, peeled back and resting on the trunk lid. The driver's door was completely gone. The place in the steering wheel where only a short time before the front air bag had been seated, was now a gaping hole as a result of the need to cut it loose by the rescuers. The lower half of the dashboard, basically everything from the speedometer on down towards the floorboard, was shattered or missing. Mom's right shoe still lay on the floor where it had been when she was so gently removed by that wonderful group of firefighters and EMT workers who, as a result of their choices to volunteer for the duty, had responded to the crash. A blessing in and of itself, that we have, in this great country of ours, men and women who, so unselfishly, volunteer to be first responders and face these situations on a daily- even, in some cases, hourly-basis.

The investigating officer introduced himself to me and I immediately recognized his voice from the cell phone conversation only a few minutes earlier. He was a thoughtful man with a soft voice that comforted both Cheryl and I as we talked to him. He was just finishing his inventory of the belongings and, after briefly going over it with us, handed us Mom's purse. In his compassionate voice he said, "She is on her way to Toledo, you'll want to get there soon." Again, he reiterated that because of how alert and talkative she was, that he didn't feel it was going to go badly for her. He didn't know at the time, none of us did, but it didn't turn out badly for her. She is with her Father God dancing in fields of grace for an audience of One.

As we traveled from the crash scene to the hospital, Cheryl and I talked some, we held hands some, but mostly we quietly prayed and thought--each in our own world of thoughts. Roads closed by trains, or by construction and every other imaginable hurdle stood in our way. And yet, there was a calm there, a peace that somehow, everything was going to be OK. The Holy Spirit was our third (first?) rider. We felt so at-ease, so comfortable with each other that neither of us realized that we had no clue where the hospital was. We didn't have the Garmin. As I mentioned, it was in our other vehicle. Again, Jehovah Jireh, the God who provides, gave my wife the idea that we should call her oldest sister whose two daughters had both gone to college in Toledo and the oldest of Cheryl's nieces had actually worked at St. V's as part of her training to be a nurse. We got great directions from her. Smooth sailing, so we were on our way down the Ohio Turnpike. God provides the right things at the right times.

My best friend, the man who was best man in our wedding, who has always been there as a steadying voice in my life was the first person I called about the crash after I left the scene. Mark answered the phone, and, after I told him what had happened and what I was going to be doing, he said, "Keep in touch, but don't worry about the animals at the farm. I'll take care of the cattle for you for as long as you need me to." Let the onslaught of blessings begin!

"Thanks Mark, I appreciate that." As I hung up, I praised the Lord again for Mark and for God's bestowing of plentiful blessings upon us. We had just received two big ones within the span of less than five minutes. He wasn't done with us yet.

At times like these, we often are blessed and don't realize until sometime later how great our God is and how he uses our situations to bring Glory to Himself. As an Athletic Director, there are a myriad of responsibilities that are required of me. One was to make arrangements to pick up track starter blanks for the upcoming track season from a coach in Cleveland. Earlier, on the day before, I had made arrangements to pick these up, and we were to meet halfway between our two schools to make the exchange. As my life-partner and I drove along in silence, I was reminded of my appointment the next day.

We have a great coaching staff in our small school. Our coaches are friendly and our kids are always at the center of our coaches' worlds. As time has gone along, I have developed a rapport with the coaches, and feel that with most of them I can ask for help when needed. One such coach is Geoff. When I realized that I probably was not going to make my appointment, I called him. After explaining what had happened and what I needed, he graciously volunteered to take care of the exchange, and assured me that we "should take care of your family stuff. Don't worry about this. You have enough to think about." Another huge blessing and one more way God used someone in our lives to comfort us. God is great!

I called my sister. Deb and I were typical older brother (by three years) and younger sister. We argued, we fought, we teased but always deep down, there was love in our house. A characteristic firmly enforced by my parents. I never realized how poor we really were until much later in my life. Because of the love in our family, we didn't notice what other kids had or we didn't have. Mom and Dad provided as best they could and always filled the house with love. We had food (much of it raised in our garden or meat from our animals), clean clothes and once I reached school age even indoor plumbing! What an exciting time in my life that was. No longer did going to the bathroom at night involve boots and a flashlight and a page or two from the Sears catalog. It was a pretty good childhood, although, I'd never have said so at the time. We were blessed then, too.

My conversation with my sister that windy and sunny late evening in March went something like this:

"Hi Bub," she said after the phone rang twice.

"Hello. Got something I need to tell you."

"Yea, what's up?"

"Mom's been in a pretty bad car crash. A guy fell asleep and went left of center and hit her head on. She's been life-flighted to St. V's in Toledo and Cheryl and I are on our way there now. The officer said he didn't feel her injuries were life-threatening."

"Do you want me to come up now?"

"No I don't think you'd have to come right now. Let me get there and see what's going on and how she is and I'll call you with an update as soon as I know anything. For now just pray that she will be OK."

"Will do, Randy, give me a call as soon as you know anything."

"OK, I will. Talk later."

"OK, love ya."

"You too. Bye"

There are times when I think my cell phone is a curse, especially when people call me about my job at the most inopportune times. But throughout this whole ordeal, it was a great thing to have. It allowed me to call family and friends and give them constant updates, which minimized the "misinformation" which so commonly surrounds an event like this. There was, very quickly, a network that formed and spread the information about Mom smoothly throughout the U. S. to all of her family, friends and acquaintances. Facebook and Twitter were not widely used then, so we went "old school" by actually talking to people! I would make three or four phone calls to key people and they would spread the information to all the others. This is something I'd highly recommend to anyone else in a similar situation. It was unbelievable how well it worked. I truly believe that, when used correctly, God's will can be accomplished, even with social media. But this time we used the simple technology of a cell phone. Mostly I wanted Mom's five siblings to have a direct line to what was happening. God used these incredible people to bless us throughout the time of the wreck, the hospital stay, the time leading up to the funeral and for several days, weeks, months and years afterward.

Mom was one of six children. She is the eldest at 79. The youngest, the only other widow in the group is Aunt Linda who is only five years older than me. Aunt Linda and I have always been fairly close, due as much to our ages as anything. She lost her husband a few years ago, just after Dad passed away. Aunt Linda talked about the "widow conversations" she and Mom would have. They grew very close in the last few years. She lives in Findlay, which is only about ½ hour from Toledo, so she came to the hospital a couple of times while we were there. It was always good to see her smiling, concerned and deeply loving face. Just being there, she was a blessing. She has been a nurse (mostly pediatric) for many years, having graduated from The Ohio State University.

We are all big "Bucks" fans in our family. One of Mom's other sisters, who also graduated from OSU worked at the branch campus in Mansfield for several years, and including myself and my wonderful wife, there are at least five or six other grads in the family. In the coming days, these folks, Miriam, Carol, Chuck, Wayne and Linda would be used by God to show His mercy and grace time and time again. We are so fortunate to have been blessed with these people and their families. There is a reason God gave us families—He knew what He was doing when He gave us this one.

The next call after my sister was to Aunt Janice (Wayne's wife). Mostly because hers was the first cell number I had in my phone. I explained what had happened and what we knew and told her that I'd call with up-dates, as I knew more. I asked her to call all the other siblings and let them know what we were doing, update them and tell them we'd keep in touch throughout the next few days as need be. She was also one of God's blessings. She works part time as a tax preparer and ultimately filed for an extension for Mom's taxes. Again, God knew what He was doing. He had it all planned and used her to His glory.

As we rode along, I continued to flash back to the time earlier in the evening when we were at the farm sitting in the living room chatting with Mom about this and that and the other thing. Seldom did our conversations involve a lot of "heavy material". Usually about her dog, King, or her great-granddaughter, Noel, or her two grand daughters, Rachel (Deb's and Michael's daughter) or Arielle (our daughter). As we were leaving I asked her what her plans were.

She said, "Well, I've been working on these darn taxes all day. I think I'll run into town and get some supper."

"OK," I said, "we'll talk to you tomorrow." I did, but I'm not sure how much she really heard of those hospital conversations. I'd like to believe that each time I talked, she knew I was there, but she always had a peaceful look on her torn and tattered face. There was never any fear of what the future would hold. God was in control. He was blessing us, and her, and that was really all that mattered. He was teaching us a lesson about faith. We were to trust in Him and not fear. We were OK with that.

CHAPTER 3

"An angel from heaven appeared to him and strengthened him"

– Luke 22:43 (NIV)

We entered the waiting room and crossed from the revolving doors across a short distance to the reception desk. As we worked our way there, I noticed that it was smaller than I expected, and a little more than half full of people waiting to see the attendants that were calling out names and directing each new patient to a room. Some patients were there by themselves, some were with a friend or family member, and some were old while others were young. A very young baby was held closely by its mother and crying as though it were hurting in every part of its body. I felt the sadness of the parents. They were hurting too. Again, feeling the sadness, I prayed a brief prayer for them while we were waiting our turn in line. "*Lord, give them a quietness to know that you are in charge, that Your Will will be done, and grant the doctors and nurses knowledge to help the little one in their care. We lay that child at Your Holy feet. Amen.*"

"May I help you…Sir, may I help you." I had gotten lost in that prayer for a moment and the poor girl behind the counter had to ask twice.

"Yes Ma'am. My mother was brought in on life-flight a little while ago. We are here now."

"Please have a seat. I'll let the chaplain know you are here." At this point, for the first time my heart sank. The Chaplain? Was she already gone and they were sending the chaplain to tell me? How was this possible? My mind raced back to the crash site. Didn't they say they thought she'd be all right? Then my thoughts again turned to God and what He is capable of. "Lord, Your Will be done." It was all I could think of.

I don't know if you could call Lanny an angel or not, but his soft, comforting voice and gentle eyes perfectly fit both a chaplain and an angel. He would become my guiding angel over the next few days. He introduced himself to Cheryl and I and explained that at St. V's the chaplains are a type of liaison between the ER doctors and the families in order that the families can be kept abreast of the workings of the Emergency Room doctors, what they are doing and how things are going. I breathed a sigh of relief. He wasn't here to tell us she was gone, just to give us periodic information about how *her treatment* was going. He began to list the plethora of injuries they had discovered since the chopper arrived. At that time, they listed a broken right arm (radius and ulna), a broken left arm (humerus), a fractured pelvis, at least two broken ribs, a skull indentation that later would be determined to be a fracture right at the bridge of her nose, a broken nose, a broken left eye orbital, and a gash extending from the center of her eyebrows down the left side of her nose to her chin. As he described each injury, one could tell he was in pain as well. He was a blessing to us, just by who he was and how he conducted himself. I don't know for sure if there are human angels on earth, but if so, he definitely proved to be one. At the very least, Lanny is a man of God with a passion for people and a gift of compassion. He had the perfect assignment at the hospital. We felt quite at ease when he finished with, " In a few minutes, I'll bring one of the doctors out to talk to you."

While we waited, I began another round of phone calls, beginning with Deb. By now it was after 10 PM, although that night I lost track of time for the most part. I hesitated to make a lot of calls at that time, but made a few critical ones anyway. Deb is a "late-nighter" while I'm an early riser. (Another of our differences that makes us who we are.) During our conversation, it was decided that she, Rachel and Noel would come up to the hospital. They would be leaving for the 2 ½ hour drive as soon as they could make arrangements, get packed and get on the road. I quietly prayed for safe travel for them.

The second call I made was to my pastor. Pastor Bob has been our pastor, friend and spiritual leader for about fifteen years. I met Bob when we chose to try a local church near our home. We had heard that this non-denominational church was growing and that, the church was led by a very strong, Bible-preaching pastor. Bob and I hit it off from our very first, "Hello!" He is a couple of months older than I, so we were raised at the same time and in similar circumstances. PB, as he is affectionately known, was raised in a Baptist home by two loving parents. His father was a Baptist minister. Mine was a Methodist home. He and I have similar likes in humor and I've relied on him over the last fifteen years for guidance in all things religious, and in life. His spirituality is remarkable and he is a great role model for me about how to live a God-centered life and how to always give without ever expecting anything in return other than the blessings God bestows hour-by-hour. When we look to God for guidance, He puts the blinders on us so we can see only His plan and His blessings, through prayer and others around us.

As the phone rang, I was a bit surprised that PB answered as quickly as he did. Although, I probably shouldn't have been, his job requires many late nights too. After a brief explanation of the events of the evening, his response was what has characterized him as a person, as a Christian and as a Pastor. "Can I pray with you over the phone?" The response was exactly what I needed. Sharing the phone with Cheryl, we sat silently with the din of the activity around us slowly fading as he lifted us, Mom, my sister's travel and many other things before the Throne. I can't tell you everything he prayed for, but it was extremely comforting as the words of a Godly man spewed forth from him in a way that put us at ease.

After the prayer, he asked what else he could do for us. In the conversation, it was discussed that we were in Toledo with only one vehicle, but Cheryl would need to get to work the next morning. "What time does she need to leave there to get to work on time?" PB asked. "She ought to be out of the hospital by 4:30 AM," I responded. That was a mere four hours or so in the future. "Why don't I grab a couple of hours of sleep, then I'll come up and get her and bring her to your home so she can get ready for school." Another of God's infinite blessings came rolling along. We agreed and ended the call. WOW, God had his hand on every detail.

Earlier as we were on the way to the hospital, feeling that no matter how things went, I'd probably not be at work the next day, I had called the secretary at my school, as well as my boss, to let them know I wouldn't be at work the next day. They were extremely gracious.

Another God sighting over the next few days were the people with whom I worked. Their constant concern and words of encouragement were astonishing. I tried to let them know how things were going too, although, I didn't do as good of a job as I should have. Our secretary always seemed very concerned and that was a blessing also. I did go to work for a few hours one of the days Mom was in the hospital just to attend to a few items that needed my immediate consideration.

Another amazing thing was that this all happened during the time between seasons just as spring sports were starting. My time was at much less of a premium during that time of the year. I know in my heart that my job is secondary to this situation, but I had always tried to be on time and at work on all the days of employment. It is a wonderful thing to be in a work setting where the people actually care for each other. We had many Christian families in our school system and many on our staff. God knew what he was doing when he put me there.

Cheryl's co-workers were very supportive also. She has taught fourth grade for 30+ years in the same school system. She loves it, loves her kids, and has excellent teachers surrounding her that supported her in Godly ways. It is the school system she attended as a child and the two women with whom she teaches are also regular attendees of our church. She relied heavily on them during that time for moral support. As our journey progressed that week, we saw each other several times, but often our contact was by phone. It was another quiet blessing to know she had them to rely upon, cry with, and pull strength from throughout the whole ordeal.

As we sat in the far corner of the ER waiting room, we finally had a couple of moments to ourselves-the first since we had arrived. We talked softly for a few minutes then she put her head on my shoulder and drifted into a light nap. I could tell because she finally began to breathe more slowly and relaxed. I just looked around the waiting room and noticed the people who were there. They had their own problems, and God and I had mine. I wondered to myself how many of them had Him to lean on as I did.

CHAPTER 4

"He heals the brokenhearted and binds up their wounds"

– Psalm 147:3 (NIV)

A half-hour or so later, Lanny returned. Telling us the "Team" was working to stabilize her and evaluate her injuries and make the plans for her treatment. At this point, it became very obvious to me that things were much more severe than first thought at the scene. As he went on, Lanny talked about the specialists that were with Mom in the ER. He talked about the hematologist, the neurologist, the cardiac specialist, the orthopedist, and some other "ists" that were involved. He said she was unconscious, but under sedation because of her condition.

As Lanny began to tell me all the doctors that were involved, I must have looked very pale. In the softest, gentlest voice on earth, he asked me if I wanted him to pray with Cheryl and I. I was sure that was exactly what we needed-Mom needed it too. Again another prayer that I could not recite was offered up for us, for our Mother, for the family as they traveled and for her siblings and their families as they awaited news. There were a lot of people she had come to know over her lifetime but some of her "special friends" would need to know soon about her condition. I decided to wait until I had more information. I would call in the morning.

Mark would be my contact. His job allowed flexibility in his schedule and I knew he'd be able to make those contacts.

When Lanny left, Cheryl and I talked. She has been my soul mate for over 32 years. God knew what he was doing when he put the two of us together. She has learned to say the right thing at the right time and not to say anything sometimes too.

"This doesn't sound good, " I said to her.

"They've got good doctors here," she said, trying to force a smile to her face, "she's in good hands."

"I know, but with all those specialists, it sounds like everything is wrong with her."

"Don't assume anything until you get to talk to one of the doctors. They should be out soon. Why don't you try to get some rest?"

"You are the one going to work tomorrow, you need to rest. Go ahead, lay your head on my shoulder and take a nap. I'll wake you when the doctors come out."

"OK, but you close your eyes too."

I told her I would, but I didn't really. I just had so many things going through my head. I drifted back to Dad's passing a couple years before. Mom had spent so much time at the hospital with him. He was in intensive care for two weeks after he had already been in the hospital for a week prior to that as a result of his last cancer surgery. She often said to me that she had "lost Dad" when he went into intensive care two weeks before he died. He never woke up again. I wondered if my last words "See you tomorrow", that I had said at the farm a few hours before, would be the last ones, or would I really see her "tomorrow". I apparently drifted off, but didn't really sleep because I was in an emergency room. The little ones were crying, the adults were being called one-by-one to go to their appointed examination rooms and the seats were very uncomfortable.

As the doors to the ER opened, I saw Lanny and a doctor approach. I knew I was about to hear life-changing news, no matter what it was. The doctor introduced himself and pulled up a chair seated directly in front of us. "I am the head of your mother's ER team. When we have severe cases like this, we bring in all the specialists and each is involved in the initial examination. I will be the lead physician, as the orthopedist, but each doctor will have input according to his or her specialty. Your mother has many internal injuries. At this point we have done some x-rays and we know that she has…"

At that point he went on to explain the entire litany of injuries. Among the things he mentioned were broken bones in virtually every part of her body, some bruising of major organs, including a skull fracture near the bridge of her nose and brain contusions. Her heart was doing fine now, but he wondered if I knew all the medicines she was on. Of course, I didn't.

I knew exactly where that list was. When Dad had gotten ill about nine years before, she started cataloging every thing about his treatments. Things like doctors' visits, medications, and conversations with all the doctors, where and when he had dialysis and mounds of other copious notes were all in one large 3-ring notebook.

I found out after Dad's passing, she had done the same for herself. One day, she shared with me that she had included all her medical cards and all the current information about her prescriptions and that it was in a notebook at the farmhouse in the desk. I knew exactly where it was, but it wasn't doing much good now. Cheryl said she could get it and bring up the next day. At that point, they informed us that if Mom did survive her injuries, she would need a lot of therapy, and might need full-time care. I appreciated his honesty. It was a statement that weighed heavily on me for the next week. He said she would be in ICU for the rest of the night and then probably undergo surgery the next day to see if they could relieve the pressure on her brain and set the broken arms and legs. The broken pelvis would have to wait until she regained some of her strength. They were going to monitor her internal organ injuries.

Lanny offered to pray with us again. The doctor said he thought that was a good idea and we all prayed together right there in the waiting room. I was so impressed that the Doctor wanted to pray with us. Lanny proceeded to pray for us, Mom, the Doctors and all the other relevant individuals involved. When he finished Doctor M shook my hand in the warmest way possible and wished us well.

After he left, Cheryl and I prayed. "*Lord, you know what is best. We don't understand your plan in all of this, but we give you all the praise and honor, knowing that you will bless us throughout the coming days and weeks. We claim your promise that you will strengthen us and that we will never face anything that You and we cannot handle together. Thank you for what You are going to do in all of this. In Your holy and precious Name we pray, Amen.*"

I called Deb to let her know what they had said. She told me they were about a half-hour away. I explained to her where to park and where to enter and told her I'd see her shortly.

It was late, but Aunt Janice had told me to call anytime. I felt the brothers and sisters needed to know that Mom was going to be there awhile. I called her to let her know what we'd been told. I asked her to let the others know that the next day (Friday) would not be a good day for any of them to visit-she was scheduled for surgery. The doctors said it would be at least five hours, however, it ended up being over eight. I was tired, nervous and antsy. I prayed for calm and peace and understanding. I felt it immediately.

The rest of that night was a blur of my sister arriving, consoling her tears and those of her daughter and granddaughter, signing papers, and trying to hold myself together as well as everyone else. It was difficult. I was worried about Alice, too. I had no way to get in touch with her daughter. As it turned out, her number was in Mom's phone. Later, when things settled down a bit, I said something about getting in contact with Joni (Alice's daughter) and Cheryl thought to look in Mom's contacts on her cell phone. She always knows what to say. Another blessing was that I had the opportunity to talk to Joni, and to see Alice later.

Around 4:00 AM, Pastor Bob arrived. By this time, they were prepping Mom for her room in ICU. When PB arrived, we filled him in on what had transpired up to that point. While he was there, the doctor returned to give us another update. Lanny was with him. I knew that again, God was blessing us in our deepest hour of need. "*Lo, though I walk through the valley of the shadow of death, I will fear no evil, for thou art with me.*" The Twenty-Third Psalm rang loud and true through my mind and thoughts. We were in the shadows, and I was feeling His comfort beside me. PB led a prayer, with all of us there; the doctor, Lanny, Cheryl, Deb, Rachel, Noel and Me. I remember I wondered if the doctor was a Christian, or if he was just humoring us. I found out later, during one of our conferences that he was a very strong Christian man. So were his assistant, a lovely young intern, and most of the nurses on Mom's floor.

Soon it was time for Cheryl to leave. We took a couple of minutes to call Arielle and update her. She wanted to know about coming to the hospital. We dissuaded her from that for the time being by telling her that we would let her know if anything changed. She and her grandmother had always been close and it was difficult for her being so far away when the rest of the family was there. We told her grandma understood and she could visit later. Before Cheryl left we took a couple of minutes to just be alone together. She held me in a hug that was so warm, kind and loving that I didn't want it to end. She whispered that things would be all right because God was in control. I knew she was right, but it was difficult to let her go. She was my biggest blessing. God really did know what he was doing when he had brought us together, nearly 35 years before. I didn't always think of her as blessing, especially when our disagreements were because I didn't get my way, but she was, and still is a blessing.

The doctor had told us she would be having surgery on Friday if she gained enough strength overnight. I had a feeling she would. She was a strong woman in all ways—mentally, emotionally, physically and spiritually.

She had retired from a long working life. She had held many jobs, but all of them were ones that utilized her strengths. She had been a bank teller for many years. That job allowed her to use her business sense. The lessons learned there would serve her well later in life when she became the Township Clerk and handled all of its finances.

From working in the bank, she went to work at the school as a study hall monitor. They still tell stories about her at the Junior High school where she worked. Her classroom was a large cafeteria that would seat over 200 students. At 5'5" tall, she was not at all an imposing figure to a Jr. High student. But the stories are told that she could command the respect of all 200 of them instantaneously when the tardy bell rang. She had "the look". I know it well, because she used it on me a lot. She had no problem utilizing the discipline of the day. If one walked into her study hall any time of the day, you might see some of the largest boys in the class standing on the wall around the room holding their books with a pained expression on their faces indicating they had been there for some time. Copying dictionaries and encyclopedias and other types of additional "busy work" were very common. The word was on the street—don't mess around in Mrs. Hord's study hall!

She had incredible organizational skills. At that time the Junior High was on a mod system. That meant that every fifteen minutes, all day long, some students were coming and going. Some students would be there any combination of 15-minute mods. Some for 15 minutes, some for 30 and some would stay for up to 45 minutes. She worked very hard at her "seating charts" so all the kids rotated in and out as their schedules required without interruption from the others. I never could figure out that organization.

As a result of working at that job, she was able to move into the treasurer's office as a secretary. From all accounts she was very efficient there as well. Eventually, she left that job and became the school secretary for one of the elementary schools in the district. She enjoyed that job because she had a lot of freedom to "run the show". The other nice thing for her was that the school was only about 4 miles from the farm and she liked the convenience. It was the same elementary school my sister and I had attended.

I spent my entire childhood attending our local United Methodist church with our family. It had started as an Evangelical United Brethren Church, but about the time I was in Jr. High, they merged with the Methodists to make the United Methodist church. The teachings were not that much different, but it was not something most in our church liked. We went every Sunday unless the weather was really bad or we were on our one-week vacation. Sunday school first, then the worship service and on Sunday evenings, once we were old enough, we went to Youth Group. We had a strong background in Christianity, led for the most part, by Mom. Her faith was extremely important to her. She had been raised in a German household with strong ties to the Lutheran church. She made sure we knew the difference between right and wrong. Sometimes, in the midst of discipline, the verse, "spare the rod and spoil the child" would get uttered. I have had trouble finding that exact paraphrase in the Bible. The closest I've ever come was from Proverbs 13:24, but that's a bit of a stretch to get it to that point. No matter, this was her philosophy of discipline for a teenage boy who didn't always make the best choices. She was strong in faith, in body, in mind and in heart. She was one of God's great works.

CHAPTER 5

"The Lord gives strength to his people; The Lord blesses his people with peace."

– Psalm 29:13 (NIV)

As Mom was settled into her ICU room, Deb wondered out loud what she should do about Noel and Rachel for the night. It was decided they would get a hotel room a few miles away where they could put the baby down and maybe get some rest themselves. Once Mom was settled, they left. Cheryl and PB had gotten away just before 4:30 AM. She would have plenty of time to get work. I talked later to Cheryl about that ride home and what they discussed. She said they chatted about several topics, but mostly, about Mom, and me, and what was about to happen. PB reminded her that it was in God's hands. She was blessed by his words. She made it to school, and was able to get through the day. Many prayers were sent up that Friday by her co-workers. She was much less stressed than I thought she might be because of them.

The nurses on Mom's floor were amazing. They were the kindest, most wonderful people in the world. I needed that, because by about 5:30, everyone else was gone and it was just me. The hospital had a policy about sleeping in the patients' rooms, but that early March morning, they made an exception and allowed me to stay in her room and rest in a chair that was at her bedside.

The room was large—much larger than I thought it would be. It was located very near the nurses' desk and the nurse assigned to her was visible as I sat in the chair. The sounds were ones I was all too familiar with from spending time with Dad during his last days. The beeps and buzzers all meant something to those that were trained, to me though, they simply meant everything was going as the medical staff expected. The nurse would come in every few minutes and check on her. I would stand and move out of the way so she had full access to Mom's bed, then sit back down and drift into a light sleep until the next round of "checks".

Soon, the ER Team Doctor-the orthopedist, came into her room. I had purposely stuck around to be there when he came in. He confirmed that Mom was going into surgery. They felt her vital signs were strong and she'd be as able to stand the surgery as well now as if we waited for a time. After hearing what he had to say, I consented to the surgery.

Mom had a living will which was another blessing on the family. As the eldest of her children, it was my responsibility to make all the decisions regarding her care. Mom and I had discussed this when Dad was bad. It was one of the many conversations we had during that time. Now those discussions were also a blessing. I knew what she wanted. I did council with my sister regularly, though, before making most of the decisions.

I called Deb to let her know what was going on. During the course of the conversation, she said she thought they would sleep a while longer, then take Noel and go shopping or something because it would not be good for her to sit there all day with nothing to do. We were playing a delicate balancing act between giving Noel enough information to help her understand what was happening to Great Grandma without scaring her. She really wanted to see her, but with the injuries, the resulting swelling and all the bandages on her face, we thought it best not to allow that.

Soon the neurologist came in to discuss the extent of the brain and other neurological injuries. Accompanying him into the room was a young female intern. As the week went on, the intern and I would have many discussions about Mom's condition. She was extremely knowledgeable and both she and the specialist had a gentleness and kindness in their voices that was very comforting.

"Hello, I'm Dr. R, the neurologist. Your mother has some pretty severe injuries to her skull and those are putting pressure on her brain," he said after first introducing his intern. "There are signs of partial paralysis that may be temporary or may be more permanent. We just don't know at this time."

"Her skull, directly above the bridge of her nose is fractured and is putting pressure on the front part of her brain. There is some bruising of her brain that is typical of severe concussions. She has some response to stimuli, but not to the level we'd like to see. She has severe trauma to her left eye, and we don't think she will be able to use it, although it is early." His statements were not what I wanted, but I sort of expected that this might be the case.

"This will be a long road to recovery if she can make it through the surgery," he finished.

"What we want to do is to get all the broken bones fixed first. That is the top priority right now," the orthopedist said. He had joined us during the discussion, but I hadn't seen him come in. "After talking with the team we can tell you this. The multiple broken bones and skull fracture-along with the resulting neurological problems are the main problems right now. Your Mother's organs are all functioning at this time and it seems that her heart and lungs are fine. We will continue to monitor those for any signs of distress."

His next statement seemed to give me some hope that everything might turn out all right.

"When we are done with the surgery, we will keep her in a drug-induced coma for a couple of days to give her body some time to rest from all the trauma. If things go as we anticipate, we will re-evaluate at that point and see where she is." Good news—I guess.

"If you are doing the surgery to repair the broken bones, are you going to do the skull fracture at the same time?" I asked.

"We are not going to do anything with it, I don't think. Like I said, we'll see how she handles the rest of the surgery. We have seen cases where those small bones move on their own and we don't have to do anything."

I must have had a pretty defeated look on my face. As the doctors left, the intern came to me and put her hand on my shoulder. "We will do everything we can to help her. Continue to pray for her, that always helps." Her face slowly drew to a smile and I was comforted and blessed by her as well.

When they had left, the nurse came in and suggested I go get something to eat. I had not eaten anything since lunch the day before, and often with the rigors of my job, lunch usually involved a "snack" on the run.

"I'm really not hungry, but I could use a place to lie down for a little while."

"There is a lounge down the hall that is being remodeled. No one is supposed to be in there, but I'm sure it would be alright for you to use it," she said to me. "I'll know where you are that way, if I need you."

After she led me out the doors of the ICU and down a short hallway, I thanked her for her help and she told me if there was anything I needed to let her know and she'd try to get it for me.

I made a couple more phone calls, because most of the people I was calling would be getting ready for work. I called Mark first to fill him in. He said he would call all the neighbors and his sister and brother-in-law, and they could contact the church family. Next, I called Aunt Janice. Taking very precise notes (I know because I repeated things so she could write them down), she let me know that she would contact all my Mother's siblings with the news. Finally, I called Deb back and filled her in on what the doctors had said. She would stay in contact with me during the day.

I laid down to rest and fell asleep. Thankfully, the couch I was sleeping on was very uncomfortable, so I woke up about an hour later, and went over to check on Mom. The nurses were in the middle of shift change. Mom's new nurse had no idea who I was. As I entered the ICU ward she noticed me and said in a very firm, demanding voice, "Hey, you can't be in here. You'll have to come back during visiting hours." I didn't try to explain what I was doing. I was so shocked that I simply said, "I'm sorry" and returned back out the way I came. I said a prayer at that moment.

"Lord, give her a special blessing today. She needs You with her right now." I don't know why I did that, I just did.

About 20 minutes later, she appeared at the door of the lounge and asked if we could talk.

"Sure," I said, "Come on in."

"I want to apologize for the way I treated you in the ICU a few minutes ago. I didn't know who you were. I'm so sorry to hear about your mother. We will do everything we can to keep her comfortable after her surgery. Would you like to see her before they take her to surgery?"

"I would, thank you."

As we walked down the hallway together, I thought of the blessings that were just pouring down on me. My eyes watered and I sniffed. God had his hand in all of this. I was seeing it more and more. I had a feeling that the best was yet to come. I wouldn't be disappointed.

CHAPTER 6

"However, as it is written, 'No eye has seen, no ear has heard, no mind has conceived what God has prepared for those who love Him'—but God has revealed it to us by his Spirit…"

– I Corinthians 2:9-10a (NIV)

Soon the orderlies came to take her to surgery. Before they came I said a prayer with Mom. It had been years since we prayed together, other than around the table before we ate a family meal. I held her bandaged left hand gently so as not to "undo" any of the many tubes to which she was attached. It was a simple prayer, but I just knew that Mom was fine with it. I asked for healing, if it be God's will, I asked for knowledge and discernment for the doctors as the surgery progressed and I asked for blessings for the entire staff at the hospital. I closed by adding safe travel for anyone that might be coming to see her in the days that followed.

When I finished, I looked up to see the nurse standing at the door, her head bowed. Behind her were the gurney and orderlies that would transport her to the operating room. It was time. I touched her forehead and kissed her gently on the cheek and stepped out of the room.

As I left I told the nurse I'd be in the lounge. She said she would come down when Mom was headed to surgery. She thought it would be about 10 or 15 minutes.

When I got to the lounge, I called Cheryl to update her. She wondered if I had eaten and asked if I had gotten any sleep. There she goes, putting me first again! I answered both questions and said once I knew exactly what I was supposed to do, I would try to get a little of both. I was still dressed in my jeans and t-shirt from the night before. I asked her when she came back up to bring me a bag, so I could take a shower, brush my teeth and change clothes. She said she would and we closed the conversation with our usual "I love you"s.

I had nothing to read or anything to do while I waited, so I closed my eyes. Floods of scriptures came flowing to mind. It was the Holy Spirit providing exactly what was needed at exactly the right time in exactly the right amounts. I must have drifted off for a while.

"Mr. Hord…Mr. Hord…" The soft voice sounded almost angelic. It was a young lady dressed in an aid's uniform. "If you come with me, I can show you where to wait so the doctors can keep you updated. They will know where you are."

"Thank you," I said and followed her to the elevators. We chatted a bit as we went along. I asked her where I could go to get something to eat and she gave me directions for where to find the cafeteria. She led me to the main entrance and a large waiting room.

"You may wait here," she said, and turned to the attendant and said, "This is Mr. Hord. His mother is in surgery." The attendant was a large man, even when he was sitting.

"Mr. Hord, just have a seat anywhere. If you need anything, just ask." His burly voice fit his size, I thought. "I'll let the operating team know you are here. This might be a good time to get something to eat if you'd like."

"Thank you, I think I will."

He repeated the directions the young lady had just given me. I wasn't really hungry, just tired. I went to the cafeteria and picked up some yogurt and fruit. "That will suffice for now," I thought.

As I moved to the checkout line, there was a young woman, probably in her mid- to late-twenties in line in front of me, trying to corral three very active young boys, while pushing a stroller with a fourth child in it, juggle their food, her food, her purse all while trying to get her wallet out to pay her bill. I offered to push the stroller for her if that would help, and she agreed, thanking me. As we waited for the man in front of her to pay, I said another prayer for her and her family. This is not the place you take your kids for a family outing, so I felt that probably she was not having the best of days. As I finished, I looked at her and she broke out in a large smile. Her beautiful, white teeth were framed by her dark, smiling face. It was almost as though the calming effect was instantaneous for her. When she had paid, she thanked me, took her brood and set off for a table near by. I was happy for her.

This period of a week with little to think about but my thoughts and God, really had a drastic effect on my life in virtually every imaginable way. I was alone, for the most part, all the time. With Cheryl at work and Deb, Rachel and Noel at the hotel, I had plenty of time to be alone, with Him. It was a phenomenal time of growth in my emotional, mental and especially my spiritual life. Our pastor had always talked about setting aside time to be "alone with Jesus". It took this experience for me to find out exactly what he'd meant. I would not be disappointed by it.

By a little after 9:00, I had taken a short nap, eaten the fruit and yogurt and had picked up a magazine from one of the tables in the large waiting room. I sat in a far corner of the room in an overstuffed couch that literally seemed to swallow me on occasion. This was an O.R. waiting room, so it was a bustle of activity, although I never felt it was particularly crowded. Small groups of people sat together and talked in hushed, but not whispering voices. Occasionally, a doctor or nurse would come out and talk to one group or the other, and shortly thereafter, they'd leave, just as another was arriving. Some, obviously, received good news as smiles and handshakes with the doctors flowed.

I do remember, however, one small group containing perhaps five people including two small children, who were not so happy. I could tell from his body language as he approached them that the doctor probably did not have good news. I watched as he led them into a small room just off the side of the room in which we sat. Shortly after he took them in, he left and they came out shoulders drooping and the younger of the two women in the group was crying hard. The little kids were hanging on to her jeans pockets as they walked down the hall. My heart broke for her. I could only imagine how hard that moment was for her. I felt moved to pray again (I know, same old story, right?). *"Lord, we don't know what has happened to that family, but we just want to offer them up to you. Quiet their hearts Lord. Let them know you are in control and that they will someday understand Your plan."* I closed my eyes and napped.

A very lovely young nurse accompanied by another of the hospital's chaplains awakened me a few minutes later.

"Mr. Hord, I'm Nurse C…I was just coming out to give you an update. We have gotten several of the bones set at this point. We are continuing to monitor your Mother's vital signs and she seems to be holding her own pretty well. She's a very strong woman. We will come back out when we finish the surgery. Do you have any questions?" I shook my head.

I felt that things were in God's hands and he had put those surgeons in that place at that time for a reason. There was nothing more I could do. At that point, the chaplain prayed with both of us, and they left.

I went to the restroom and returned to where I had "camped out" four hours earlier. It seemed like they were on the downhill side now. As I sat and thought and reminisced about my childhood, I distinctly remembered our old farmhouse we had lived in when I was young. I remembered how cold it was because the central heat was a pot-bellied stove in the center of the house, with a register located directly above it that led into my parents' room.

My "bedroom" was the wide landing at the top of the stairs. There was just enough room for a twin bed along the wall and a dresser at one end. I even remembered the night I rolled out of bed, off the landing and down the steps. When Mom got there, she held me close and warm. I felt that warmth right at that moment. Memories are one of the greatest gifts God gives us to console and protect us at times like these. It was a good memory and I sucked it all in. Another of God's great blessings sent my way just when I needed it. But, He wasn't done with me yet!

I leaned forward in my chair and was as relaxed as it was possible to be, when suddenly, a strong wind blew against me. It was strong enough that it physically moved me back against the chair, but there were no doors or windows open. It was as though some one had blasted me in the sternum with a forearm.

"I want you to write me a book. I want you to call it 'Journey of Praise'. I want you to tell people what I'm doing for you and those around you. Tell them about the blessings I'm giving you."

I looked around to see who was talking. There was no one within 30 feet of me. I couldn't figure out who had just spoken to me. It was an audible voice loud enough that I could actually hear it. I am very literalist in my thoughts. I would often tell PB (quite to his chagrin) that I couldn't find a single verse in the Bible with my name in it, therefore, how was I supposed to know what God wanted *me* to do? So, the thought that God, through his Holy Spirit, was speaking to me, went against everything I thought I knew about how He operates. This began the process by which this book came to be. In our darkest hours, God sends signs and comfort in ways we cannot even imagine. This book is designed to fulfill that command from God. The blessings have not stopped since, or maybe I'm just noticing them more.

I sat and tears came down my face. I grabbed a tissue from the box on the table nearby and wiped them away. I blew my nose and got up to throw the used tissue away. As I was walking back to my "camping spot" another young nurse came toward me. The conversation went something like this.

"Mr. Hord?"

"Yes, Dear."

"Hello, I'm Nurse N…Your Mother's surgery is going well. The doctors believe they will be finished with what they wanted to accomplish within about a half hour."

"Good, it sounds like things are going well," I replied.

"They would like me to take you upstairs to see Dr. N. He is a plastic surgeon. They'd like for you to talk with him right away."

Suddenly, I was concerned that something else had been discovered and that they had bad news for me. "OK, let's go," I said. As we headed toward the elevator, I said another prayer, similar to the ones I'd been praying since the whole ordeal started.

"Lord, I don't know what you have in store now, but Your Will be done and help me make the right decisions that bring Glory to You. Thank You for all we've been through and for what is still to come."

As we stepped out of the elevator, I saw a nurses' station and sitting at it was a distinguished looking man in a lab coat. It was the plastic surgeon I had been summoned to see.

"Hello Mr. Hord. I wanted to give you an update on your Mother and to discuss our next steps. Your Mother is doing well in surgery. She is very strong for her age and is tolerating everything very well. We'd like to do some plastic surgery on her face. There are two things we'd like to do. We'd like to see if we can make the large cut on her face a little less noticeable, but more importantly, we'd like to see if we can do some work on the bone at the top of her nose and see if we can get it to come back out and relieve some of the pressure on her brain. We have had patients where simply opening the skin and lightly manipulating the broken bone underneath causes it re-align and take the pressure off the under side tissues."

"WOW, not what I expected," was all I could say. I thought for a minute and decided that if it had any chance of preventing any further brain damage, it was worth a shot. I know enough anatomy of the brain to be dangerous, but I do know that the front of the brain is extremely important and that if the damage caused more swelling, that would be very harmful.

"Sure, go ahead. Do whatever you need to."

"Thank you, I believe it's a good choice. We'll let you know how things are going when we finish. It will probably be a couple of hours or so."

I excused myself with the usual niceties and the nurse returned me to my "camp". I sat down and just allowed myself to relax and get swallowed up by the overstuffed chair. I called Cheryl and Deb to let them know what was going on. They both were glad I had called. I would call Aunt Janice in a few minutes when I knew she would be home from work. It was just after two, and she got home around 3:30. I fell asleep. I rested very well, albeit, only for a few minutes. God is good, I thought. He truly is.

CHAPTER 7

"Lord, my God. I called you for help and you healed me...Sing the praises of the Lord, you his faithful people; praise His holy name."

– Psalm 30:2 & 4 (NIV)

I was startled awake by a familiar little voice. It was Noel. Deb and Rachel had come back to the hospital to see how things were going. We talked for a while. Deb asked if I was hungry and wanted to get something to eat. I told her I wanted to wait until the surgery was finished, but I could use something to drink if she was going to the cafeteria. She thought they would, but just as they were ready to leave, a familiar figure approached. It was Lanny. He sat down and I made all the introductions. He said he was on his "rounds" and saw me and wanted to stop and chat for a moment.

After filling him in with what had transpired during the day, he asked if he could pray with us. Again, his calming voice came through and struck deep in my heart. He was truly a gift from God and God had called him for just the right ministry. When he had finished, he asked if there was anything I needed. I told him Cheryl was coming later with a bag of clothes and I would need a shower. He told me he would stop by the ICU nurses' station and make the arrangements with them. He also mentioned a program they had at this hospital called "Home Away from Home."

Many years ago, St. Vincent's was a nurses' college with on-campus housing. Much of that is gone now, but a few of the old dorm rooms were left as part of one wing of the hospital. Lanny told me it was operated by the chaplains' association to provide housing for families of patients who lived too far away to travel each day. It is a free service, but they do request a donation for upkeep. After inquiring whether there was any room, he told me he would check on that too and get back to me. As it turned out, there were no rooms available for the weekend. That was fine. God would provide—I just knew he would.

Lanny dismissed himself with a promise to check in on me later. It was so comforting to feel like I had someone who was dedicated to helping me get through such a difficult time. Deb took the girls and went to the cafeteria while I waited to hear from the surgical team. I didn't have to wait long. Dr. N came through the elevator doors and walked directly to my camp. The conversation was something like this.

"Mr. Hord, your mother will be back in her room in ICU shortly. You'll be able to see her there. We were able to set all the broken bones except her pelvis. That is pretty badly broken. It will take some surgeries later to fix that."

"Surgeries? More than one?" I thought.

"She's had enough for today. As for the plastic surgery, we were able to stitch her face and, even though there will be a scar, it won't be terrible. We were not able though, to get the broken bone on her skull to retract back to its normal position. Sometimes, over time, these things will fix themselves. In the mean time, we are going to monitor her brain waves closely. There is still a lot of swelling on her brain and she will not be regaining consciousness any time soon. We'd like to keep her in a coma for the time being to give her body a chance to rest and recuperate. Do you have any other questions for me?"

I answered that I thought he had pretty well covered it and he excused himself.

Deb and the girls had come back in the meantime, and we prayed. All four of us participated, including Noel. *"Help Great-Grandma get better so we can read stories together,"* was her simple and poignant prayer. From the mouths of babes often comes great insight.

We talked as we walked through the hospital to the elevators that would take us to ICU. Deb asked if I had called the family yet to let them know, and I told her I would do so as soon as Mom was back in her room. It would give Deb a little alone time with Mom and Rachel and Noel could go with me back to my space in the ICU waiting room. I began to realize as we walked that this was going to be an even longer haul than I first imagined, and the prognosis did not sound as good as it had just 18 hours before. I prayed for the will of God to be done. That's all I had to go on now. It would be a long week.

I called Aunt Linda this time, just to spread it out a little bit. I let her know about all the details that I knew relative to the surgery and injuries. Her nursing background made this a good call, because she was able to understand, in detail, all the things I was describing. God's hand on me again. It was fast becoming overwhelming.

As the evening went on, I became aware that I hadn't touched base with Mark or Don lately. I called them to fill them in on what had gone on that day and the early prognosis. Even if she survived, I had told them, it would be a long road to recovery. I knew that she would need months of therapy, and might not ever be completely as she was before the surgery. I had resigned myself to the future with her if that was what God had planned.

After I finished the calls, I walked back into ICU to check in on Mom. Her nurse updated me with all the things I needed to know. For the first time, I saw my mother as a weak and frail woman. She had never been like that before. She'd always been so strong, alert, alive and vivacious. She looked tattered and torn. I didn't see her face anymore, I saw someone different—someone I almost didn't recognize. I smiled as I thought of some of my shenanigans when I was younger, but seeing her like that still hurt. I prayed for God to quiet my heart and to do His work in her, whatever that may be. Look out; here comes another blessing.

As I sat and drifted between the present, the past, the book I was reading and the future, and chatted with Deb, time passed slowly. The nurses came in occasionally, asked if there was anything I needed, checked on various screens and gadgets that were attached to Mom, then left me again. I rested, and slipped in and out of awareness of my surroundings for a couple of hours. I was snapped out of my daydreaming by the shuffle of feet and familiar voices. It was my lovely bride, her father, Richard and her older sister, Kim.

Dick was quite a character. I'm not sure he was ever willing to admit his age, and that he was not the "he-man" he had once been. When he found out that Cheryl needed to come back to the hospital for the weekend, he offered to drive her up Friday night and drive back to his home that night. The two-hour drive each direction was more than any 79-year-old man should do. Kim volunteered to ride along and "help with the driving", although we all knew he'd never allow anyone else to drive his truck if he was in it.

It was good to see Cheryl. I had missed her so much that day. Her counsel and her ability to know exactly what to say and when to say it would have been very helpful. She arrived with a change of clothes and the necessary toiletries to take a shower. There was a small shower room directly across the hall from the waiting room that I was staying in. Cheryl sat and chatted with Deb, Rachel and Noel and Kim and Dick, while I took a shower. I had not been more refreshed by a shower in a long time, and although I had not slept much, I didn't feel overly tired either. God's strength was filling me and I knew that He would not give me more than I could handle. He promised it to us, I believe it because I had now experienced it. I hope, and pray, that you do to, if you haven't already.

A little later, Deb decided that she and the girls would return to Columbus. Her husband, Michael worked nights and she wanted to get back before he left. Although they had driven Rachel's car, they only had one vehicle and he would need it for work. I told her I'd call if there were any updates. In the meantime, she should take care of things at home and not worry. I kissed her and the girls goodbye, wished them safe travel and walked them to the elevator. She said they'd probably be back on Sunday afternoon, if nothing came up between then and now. Nothing did. It was good for her to be home with Noel. The child needed a sense of normalcy in her life. She couldn't understand why she was not allowed to see Great-Grandma. Deb and I both felt that seeing her Great-Grandma in that situation was not good for her. Noel needed to remember her without all the bandages, tubes, cuts and scrapes. It turned out, that was a good decision. Again, God had his hand in the smallest details and the largest decisions. Blessings rained down on us.

As we returned to the ICU, I talked about the things Mom had been through that day. The many changes in game plans during the course of the surgery and the way she looked so frail. Cheryl commented that she thought Mom looked surprisingly well, considering it all. Like I said, she always knew what to say. In all of this, Cheryl was my biggest blessing. God didn't make a mistake over thirty years prior in putting us together. He knew I would need her now, and I did. It had been that way throughout our lifetime together. Praise God for her.

As we sat in Mom's room, Aunt Linda appeared at the door with Uncle Wayne and Aunt Janice. It was exactly *what* I needed exactly *when* I needed it. They were there. Aunt Linda had not told me when I talked to her earlier that they were coming, nor that Aunt Janice and Uncle Wayne would be with her.

Wayne and Linda had always been close, more because of their similarity in age than anything else. I remember when I was young standing in the front yard of my Grandparents home, hearing a ruckus from inside, and suddenly the screen door burst open and out came Linda on a full run with Wayne right after her. Just as she cleared the front door frame I saw the lower half of Wayne's leg with one of his black boots flying toward her posterior. He missed, but I was convinced that, because of her size, if it had landed, she might well have traveled the full twenty yards to the road in the air as a result of the contact. She was smaller, and a little faster than he, so she got away without any damage done. I smiled as that thought crossed my mind looking at them standing in the door.

I gave them a little more of an update while we stood by the bedside. I was able to point to various parts of her body and face as I discussed what I knew about the surgery. I told them I fully expected one of her doctors to arrive soon to give me a rundown of the day's events and the future. We didn't wait long. Mom's neurologist and his intern appeared a short time later, and, after brief introductions, gave us the information he had at the time.

He felt the surgery had gone well. Mom was strong and had come through in relatively good condition. They were concerned, though, about the concussion and fracture in the front of her skull. They were afraid that if that couldn't be repaired, or if it didn't move on its own, there could be permanent brain damage. Because it involved the Frontal Lobe of the brain, he believed that even if she survived, she would not have full body function as she had before. Some therapy would help, but she'd probably be living in an assisted living situation, at least for the near future. It was good for some of her family to be there when I got this news. They surrounded me and loved on me. That was a blessing also.

The news was scary. I hadn't even thought of the possibility that she might not go to her home on the farm. She had always fought like crazy to stay there. I had been talking to her since Dad passed away about getting a condo in town, near many of her friends. Someplace she didn't need to worry about yard work or shoveling snow. She'd have none of that. She was set in her ways and nothing I could say would change her mind about leaving her home. Now, everything pointed to the fact that she probably would not be there for a very long time—if at all. It saddened me a bit.

After the doctors left, we all moved to my "hideout" and sat there to chat and relax. Aunt Linda, Uncle Wayne and Aunt Janice all left about an hour later with loving words and hugs and kisses all around. They were terrific. It meant a lot for them to have come. Kim, Dick and Cheryl had not eaten yet, and I realized that in the hustle and bustle of the day, I hadn't had much to eat either. We decided to go to a nearby Burger King and get something to eat. In his usual fashion, Dick bought our meals. Another blessing, since I hadn't taken the time to find an ATM at which I could pick up some cash. I had about two dollars left in my wallet and some change in the pocket of my jeans.

When he left that night, we shook hands. Dick put 2-$50 bills in my hand, saying, "Just in case you need something." I thanked him and said goodbye to him and Kim. Cheryl walked them out to their car to get her things and I went back to the Intensive Care Unit via the elevator. It would be a long night, but better because Cheryl and I were together. About 10:30, I told the nurse that I was going to go get some rest, and she assured me that was a good idea. She knew where to find me if she needed to. She asked if there was anything I needed. I asked her if I could have a pillow and a blanket. She made arrangements for me to get one of each. Cheryl and I went to the waiting room and sat together under the blanket and dozed for the night. It felt good to have her there. God had filled a busy day with many blessings, but He'd saved the best for last. I actually slept fairly well given the circumstances.

I woke about 5:30 in the morning and walked the short distance from my "bedroom" to the ICU. The same nurse was on duty as when I'd left the night before, but she said shift change was at 6 AM. I hung around to meet the day nurse. It was the same one as yesterday. I felt good about that, because at this point, I too needed some stability. After all the usual checks and record keeping, the nurse came back in to Mom's room to check on me. I asked how the night had gone and she said there was little change but that all the vital signs looked good. Mom was holding her own.

In the meantime, Cheryl had joined me in the room. A young man, tall, dark and strongly built showed up soon after I had settled in. Mom's nurse told me he was there to help change the bed. She asked me if I'd like to go get some breakfast while they did that. Cheryl thought that was a good idea, so off we went to the cafeteria again. Don't get me wrong, the food in St. V's cafeteria is very good and well prepared, but by later in the week, I would be ready for something else, that, however, is a whole different story.

After breakfast, Cheryl and I took a walk outside. There is a small memorial rock garden just outside the main entrance to which we gravitated. It was warming up nicely. I still felt comfortable in a light jacket, but the sun was shining and even in downtown Toledo, it seemed every bird in town was happy and singing. God has blessed us with their songs, chirps and noises for our enjoyment, if we just take the time to notice. We chatted about a lot of things, but nothing of great significance. We called Arielle, our daughter, to let her know how Grandma was doing. I also made all the usual calls to spread the word concerning Mom's night.

As we sat and talked, I was struck by the awesome ways God puts the correct people in our lives for just the right reasons. My incredible wife was given to me for just this very time in my life. His omniscience in knowing what we are going to face and what our weaknesses will be thirty, forty or fifty years after we are born, surpasses all understanding.

We sat in silence for a while and then Cheryl softly said, "You OK?" That is our way of asking each other, "What are you thinking about?"

I told her I was, but that all the things that had happened, all the gifts and blessings we'd received, and all of God's greatness was getting to be too much. I began to cry. She gently laid her hand on the side of my head and pulled me to her shoulder and I wrapped my arms around her waist.

"I love you, and I'm glad God put you in my life," I said as the sniffles continued.

"He knew what he was doing, huh?" she said with a little giggle and through sniffles of her own.

We sat there for quite a while, just enjoying the warmth and comfort of the sun and each other's embraces. I hadn't felt this close to her and God in a long time. We weren't finished with the blessings yet.

Deb called soon after to inquire how things were going. She said that she and Michael and "the kids" (Rachel and Noel) were coming up for the day and would be there later. They would probably not be spending the night though, because Michael had to preach Sunday morning. I told her I would probably be staying at the hospital again that night and that Cheryl would be there, but she would be going home Sunday so she could go to work on Monday. I still wasn't sure how she would do that, since we still only had one vehicle in Toledo. I knew though, that God would work it out; He always did.

CHAPTER 8

"And we know that in all things God works for the good of those who love Him, who have been called according to His purpose."

– Romans 8:28 (NIV)

The rest of Saturday was the usual parade of doctors, nurses, nursing assistants and lab techs, each with his or her, own assignment. I was so struck by each person's professionalism. It was all about Mom. It was about making *her* comfortable, about *her* progress, about *her* condition. It was amazing. Each person who entered her room was kind, considerate and compassionate. The nurses were devoted entirely to her care, and they were always there anytime the machines made any kind of different tone. I paused and thanked God for each one. One of the nurses even commented about how contented we all were about everything that had happened and was happening. I told her to check out Romans 8:28.

Cheryl and I sat by Mom's bedside throughout the morning and into the early afternoon. As time went on, we would read for a while, then nap, then read some more, go for a short walk down the hall, then come back and sit some more.

At one point, we decided to find Alice and have a chat with her. We had found out through the grapevine, to which hospital she had been admitted, and how to get there. We had an enjoyable time with her and her daughter Joni. We talked about Alice's future and that she would be staying at Joni's for a while after she was released from the hospital. Alice apologized that she wouldn't be able to see Mom before she went back to Cleveland with Joni. I told her it was all right, and that I would let Mom know that she would stop by later. Alice did cry a bit when she brought up the topic of the wreck. She said she felt so helpless and that Mom had needed her, and she couldn't help. We all prayed and Cheryl and I excused ourselves and left Alice in Joni's capable hands.

After we returned to St. V's and settled back down in Mom's room, the routine was interrupted mid-afternoon as Deb came in and said, "Look who I found!" It was Aunt Miriam and Uncle Ben. Aunt Miriam was Mom's next younger sister. It was good to see them. I should not have been surprised, but I was a little.

I went through the explanation again of everything that had transpired in the just-over-48-hours since the wreck. I explained all the surgeries, the consultations with doctors, the changes and improvements or lack thereof in her condition.

I was really touched when Aunt Miriam walked to her bedside and held Mom's hand. I wondered how many times they had done that when they were young children back on the farm. My mind wandered for a bit to imagine them in their little dresses walking across the pasture on the way to the barn to gather eggs or feed the animals. They had always been close, but it was a fairly large family by today's standards. There had been four girls and two boys. I imagined that probably Mom and Miriam had always been close. As I looked in Aunt Miriam's eyes, I saw the concern and deep, deep love that had come from a lifetime of being sisters, and friends. She wasn't crying, but there was a tremendous sadness that penetrated deeply into her soul. I tried to lighten the mood a bit with a weak attempt at humor—but I was not very successful. Soon her sadness passed from her face and we continued our conversation.

They had been there a few minutes, when I heard another set of familiar voices. It was Aunt Carol and Uncle Bob. When I was growing up, I was probably closer to them than any of the other Aunts or Uncles on Mom's side.

Uncle Bob raised show pigs and so did my Dad and I. We took the animals to all the local county fairs and the Ohio State Fair. Uncle Bob had Spotted Poland China (now called "Spots"), as did we. So we would buy and sell from each other and other breeders we both knew. By running the "fair circuit" together, I really got to know them well. Their oldest son was a little over a year younger than me, so we became good friends. Denny and I were inseparable for most of the summers as we traveled from fair to fair. My maternal Grandfather also showed hogs and we all had quite a time going from one fair to the next together. As I paused for a minute and thought about that, I received another blessing, the great family we had when I was growing up. I wished that for every kid in today's world.

When Bob and Carol showed up I felt a pang of sadness for them also. Aunt Carol was the next younger of Mom's sisters and had worked at the Ohio State University in Mansfield for several years. The branch campus in Mansfield is the one from which I had graduated and Cheryl had too. Aunt Carol and I always had that in common.

They approached the bed and Aunt Carol commented about the large gash on Mom's face. I told her that the surgeons had said they could do plastic surgery when she was well enough and most of that would be gone. Everyone in the room nodded and commented about that news. Aunt Carol seemed for a few moments to be lost in her memories, also. Her face deepened in sadness too and I wondered what memories she had, or what thoughts were coming to the surface. It was truly a blessing to have this much family here again. It felt like I had so much support and help. It was going to be a good day, at least, until they all left.

We had a nice visit. Eventually, the nurses came in and wanted to do some work, so we retired to my "room", and just sat and talked. By this point, I had heard some sketchy details about the gentleman that had hit Mom, so I relayed those to the entourage.

He is a strong family man. Four children of his own, one more they adopted and one as a foster child. I found out later that he and his wife had raised several foster children and that they were considered among the best foster parents in the county. Incredibly, they would later adopt two more young boys. I also learned since then the strength of his faith and that of his wife. Another blessing was that they attend church with Mark. God gave me an outlet to know how he was doing without directly calling him.

As soon as the nurses had finished, one of the young aides came down to tell us we could go back up to the room. We all traveled there together. As we were walking, I was following the group, listening to the conversations, and was intrigued to hear them all talking about the future for Mom. They all seemed to be hoping, if only in their own minds, things were going to improve. We had no way of knowing then what God had planned. It was still wonderful to have them all here. I was sure Mom was pleased too.

As the afternoon wore on into the evening, each group began excusing themselves one at a time, until it was just Deb's family, and Cheryl and I. She asked what we were doing about dinner, and I told her we'd probably get something in the cafeteria and she inquired if we wanted to go there and eat together before they had to go. I glanced at Cheryl and we agreed.

Deb is a blessing too. We haven't always seen been on the same page on some things throughout our lives but we have done better recently. She exudes warmth just with her presence. She is a strong woman of God and is constantly reaching out to help people when they need it. She knew I needed some of that now. As we sat at the table we prayed a blessing for the meal, and for the doctors and nurses in the hospital, and for the cafeteria workers. When we were finished I felt, physically, like someone came along and lifted a huge boulder from my shoulders. I had been praying on a pretty consistent basis since the whole ordeal began, but I realized, that, other than the brief prayers with Lanny and PB, I hadn't prayed out loud with anyone. It felt right. It felt good. I felt another blessing in that moment.

We had a very light-hearted meal in the cafeteria. Deb's husband and I have a similar sense of humor and often go off on a 5 or 10 minute "escapade" of humor, each playing off the other's previous line. It was joy when I needed joy.

"More blessings; when will it ever stop?" I thought. I knew the answer, but the realization hit me like a ton of bricks.

"***I'm in control. I've got you covered***," was the answer. It was God speaking to my heart.

Once we finished eating, we slowly strolled back to the elevators. Deb and Michael had chosen to leave Noel with some friends, so we were all able to go to see Mom, together, before they left. Deb chatted with her a bit, and I noticed the sadness in her face. It reminded me of Aunt Miriam and Aunt Carol and their sadness. I stood back a ways in order to give her some time to herself. I talked to Mike and Rachel, and when Deb was done, Rachel took her turn. It pained Rachel that as she talked, Mom didn't respond. They had always been so close.

After each one had said his or her piece, we all headed back out of the ICU. It had been a good day. It had been a nice day for me, full of family, chatter, love, humor and a few tears along the way. I was glad Cheryl was spending that Saturday night with me at the hospital. I needed her warmth, her cheer, her kind words and her loving eyes to help me through another night.

About 8:30, one of the chaplains showed up in Mom's room. It wasn't Lanny, but I recognized the badge and knew what it represented. She was there to ask if there was anything I needed. I asked her if any of the "Home Away From Home" rooms were available yet. She told me she would check, but the last she knew they were still all occupied. She excused herself, retired to the nurses' desk and I heard her talking softly on the phone. She returned a few minutes later to let me know that there would not be any available for at least a couple of nights. I thanked her and she prayed with us before leaving. I guess that meant another night for Cheryl and I on the couch in the lounge. There were worse things. We said our goodnights to Mom and the night nurse and went down to my "room". It had been a long two days. But, by the Grace of God, we had made it thus far, and would, by His Grace, make it through the rest. Cheryl and I chatted a bit, and soon dozed off. We were awakened by the sound of footsteps in the hallway. One of the nurses came in carrying an extra pillow and blanket for us. Another blessing!

Chapter 9

"You, my brothers and sisters, were called to be free…serve one another humbly in love."

– Galatians 5:13 (NIV)

I awoke from a fitful night's sleep around 6 AM. I told Cheryl I was going to go down and check on Mom, and that she should try to get some more sleep.

"I'll go with you," she said softly.

We folded the blankets and put them in one of the small cupboards along with our pillows. We walked the short hallway to the ICU. As I pushed the large button on the wall, which usually opened the door, nothing happened. A voice came across a small speaker.

"May I help you?"

"I'm here to see Marilyn," I answered, almost inquisitively.

"Visiting hours haven't started yet," was the retort. I was surprised, because this had not happened before. I'd always been able to come and go as I pleased.

A different voice came over the speaker. "Come on in, Mr. Hord."

Given the situation with Mom, I had been given special visitation rights. I didn't know they were special, nor, apparently did the nurse who initially responded to my first attempt to get in. Mom's nurse let me know that the other nurse wasn't aware of the situation and now understood that I would be allowed in whenever necessary. We discussed how the night had gone. Mom was holding her own, maybe even progressing a little. They had seen some slight signs of reaction to pain when they prodded her gently on her foot.

At times like these we tend to look for little things to encourage us. That was encouraging, albeit, very minor. But I felt that the progress was enough to lighten my spirit. In retrospect, knowing what I know now, I should have been more analytical than I was at the time. I knew just enough anatomy to be dangerous, and all the years of teaching biology, health and other sciences should have made me more aware of the reality of the situation, but it didn't. I still wanted Mom to wake up, smile at me, and say "Hi Son, how are things at the farm?" I was still trying to be in control of the situation. God had her in His hands and was taking care of everything. I just wasn't willing to let Him run the whole show yet. I would learn that, too.

Cheryl and I went to breakfast at about 6:30 that Sunday morning. I wanted to go early, because the nurses told me the doctor would be in about 8:00 for his rounds. We got back from breakfast and about 8:45, Doctor R, the neurologist that had been part of the ER team when Mom was first admitted came in. He was followed closely by his intern.

"We are pleased with the way your Mother came through the surgery. She is very strong for her age." He had opened the conversation in a way that led me to believe there was more to the story.

As he reviewed the diagnosis, surgery, and prognosis, I noticed he was choosing his words very carefully. He spoke of the "short-term" rather than saying anything about the "long-term".

"There are some good signs," he said, as he enumerated the various vitals that indicated a reason to be positive.

"There are also some things we will need to watch very closely. Among those will be her brain activity."

"I take it that has not improved much," I inquired.

"Her brain activity has stabilized and is alright for now, but we have to keep a close eye on the swelling. That is her biggest enemy at this point," commented the intern. She was of Asian descent, and her large brown eyes showed a deep sense of compassion. Over the next couple of days, she became the doctor I talked to the most. I had every confidence in her and she had to be a woman of God because as they left, she asked if she could pray with me and we did. It was another unexpected blessing. What a wonderful God-filled hospital this place was. They actually believe that the doctors and nurses can't do it all—it takes a lot of help from the Almighty Lord and Savior.

For the rest of Sunday morning Cheryl and I spent our time chatting, reminiscing, laughing and crying together. It was a very special time for me. With her there, I was more relaxed than I had been since Thursday night when this journey started. She never initiated any part of the conversation. It was all about what I wanted or needed to talk about. That was an incredible blessing that God poured out as well.

There was, for the rest of the morning, the usual routine of nurses in and out, lab technicians drawing blood, and an occasional person passing by headed to another room in the ICU. The set-up was common to many of the more modern ICU's—a configuration with which I've become all too familiar. The nurses' station was semi-circular in the center of the very spacious ward. What appeared to be a workroom or break room was separated from the main room by solid walls behind the desks at which each nurse sat. Equipped with a computer workstation each one had constant visual contact with the one or two patients for which he or she was responsible. The very large patients room were situated around the exterior of the ICU ward. Each of the rooms had large windows, which could allow a great deal of natural light in when desired. I'm sure it would have been possible to get two patients in beds in each room, but the solitude of having Mom alone in one, was very comforting. The addition of a couple of comfortable chairs for Cheryl and me, made it even better.

Around noon, the ICU nurse came in and suggested we get some lunch as they were planning to change her bed and clean her up. I thought to myself, "Mom will like that." She had always been very self-aware of her looks and cleanliness, and I'm sure that if she had been able to, she would have requested just that. So, off we went to the cafeteria.

"It will take us about a half-hour," said Nurse S as we left. "Take your time."

"Thank you," was Cheryl's response, as I checked my watch. Not so much to keep them to a schedule, as much as so we didn't return too soon.

"Hungry?" I asked my lovely bride.

"Not much, but I could use a little something."

"Yea, me too."

As we walked, I thought of the servants' hearts each person with whom we had come into contact in this place seemed to have. The verse from Galatians came to mind. They truly were humble servants. Even the folks in the cafeteria seemed to respect what people might be going through, and "humbly served" both food and people. I felt blessed again by this place, its people and its attitude.

The early afternoon passed and about 2:30 Aunt Linda, Uncle Wayne, and Aunt Janice reappeared at the door. Not long after that, so did Aunt Carol and Uncle Bob. Around 3:30 Deb walked in and said that Michael, Rachel and Noel were waiting in the Lounge where we had all met prior. We all sauntered our way down there and had quite a time of socializing for a couple of hours. Another blessing came raining down, because we had not all been there together, at the same time, since our adventure had started. God's guidance, once again, manifested itself by bringing them all together. We called Arielle and all had a nice "conference" call with her. God used the technology to quiet her heart and mind also.

Among the topics discussed was how Cheryl was going to get home for school the next morning. After offers from Uncle Bob and Aunt Carol, and Uncle Wayne and Aunt Janice, it was decided that I would go home, go to work the next morning for a while and then come back in the afternoon on Monday. As each group dismissed themselves, they went to visit Mom on the way out. We stayed in the Lounge to allow them all their own "alone time" with her. Each, in turn, came back to say "Good bye" and the usual hugs and pleasantries were exchanged. Noel still wanted to go see

Great Grandma, but we told her Great Grandma was sleeping and wouldn't be able to talk to her. That seemed to suffice the child for the time being. Soon they were all gone and Cheryl and I were there together. It was great to see them all but it was good to be with just Cheryl again.

Shortly thereafter, a different chaplain appeared and told me that one of the "Home Away from Home" rooms would be available that night if I were still interested in it. I told her I was and she showed me how to get there. It was a nice place. The entrance to the facility had a large commons area where there was a small kitchen with a microwave, a stove, a sink and a few cupboards. There was also a play area for little ones that had toys strewn about. Located near the large spacious windows on one side was a table with four chairs and a rather large couch. The space was painted in light pastel colors and was bright and cheery. Exactly what I needed, exactly when I needed it.

The chaplain gave me a quick rundown of the rules and showed me around the apartment. There was a nice double bed, a large chair that reclined to make another sleeping space and a small efficiency bathroom with a shower. I couldn't wait to utilize that shower. The chaplain handed me the key and slipped out the door. "*Thank you Lord, for your provision in our time of need.*"

I said to Cheryl, "Since we have this space, let's stay here tonight. We can get up early in the morning and go home to get ready for school."

"That's a good idea. You look so tired, I'm not sure you should drive tonight anyway."

With that it was decided. We walked back to the ICU to check on Mom one more time. I double-checked to make sure the nurses had my cell phone number and the number of my room. The nurse said they were all set with both. My incredible wife and I returned to our room to sleep. It was about 10 PM so I called Mark to let him know how things were going and then turned off the lights. As I fell asleep that night, I thought of all the people here, at the hospital, that God had brought along our path. They were great servants and wonderful people. *"Mom couldn't be in a better place,"* I prayed, *"Thank you Lord for what you have done and what you will be doing."* It was a good night's sleep.

CHAPTER 10

"For I am the Lord, your God, who takes hold
of your right hand and says to you, Do not fear;
I will help you."

– Isaiah 41:13 (NIV)

We arose around 4:00 AM Monday morning and walked down to check on Mom before we left. By 4:30, we were on the road again, headed home. Traffic was light and we made good time. I encouraged Cheryl to sleep, but she said she was fine, so we just talked on the way home. It was the first I had been behind the wheel in several days other than the short trip to see Alice. My thoughts were with Mom, but it was good to get out of the hospital for a while. As we approached our hometown, Cheryl's phone rang. It was Arielle. She and her mother discussed Mom's condition. I have made a concerted effort not to talk on the phone when I'm driving if there is someone else that can talk instead. Although, with the advent of Bluetooth, I have found that it makes it much easier to use the phone when necessary.

It was decided that I would return to Toledo that night and that Cheryl and Arielle would work Monday and Tuesday and come to the hospital on Tuesday night when Arielle got off work. It would take her about 4 ½ hours to get to our house from Barboursville, West Virginia where she worked, after which she and Cheryl would make the hour and a half drive to the hospital in Toledo together. Arielle was going to be there for the rest of the time, although we didn't know that at the time. God had put on Arielle's heart and mind that she needed to be home. She took a couple days off work. It was a good thing she did.

Our daughter is a lovely young woman of God. She has found a great deal of strength and determination through daily prayer and staying close to Him. We are absolutely convinced that the young man who has become so close to her heart was put in her life by God and that they will have a long and enjoyable life together.

As we were traveling eastward on our way home that late March morning, I was struck by the beauty of the sunrise. Mom would often call me on my way to work in the mornings to ask me if I could see the sunrise. I really believe it was her favorite time of day. She loved the mornings. When we were kids on summer break, she would rise early and go to the garden at daybreak to work at pulling weeds or hoeing the vegetables before she got ready for work. She always told us it was because it was so much cooler in the morning, but I figured out early on that she just loved the mornings. The renewal of each day seemed to rejuvenate her soul and mind. She continued to be an early riser even later in life when the garden was smaller and no one else was around.

She didn't live by the motto, "Early to bed and early to rise" either. During the time Deb and I were in school, my mother, who was quite a seamstress, would pull "all-nighters" to make wedding and bridesmaid's gowns for several of the girls in our community in addition to working her regular job. I recall one particularly large wedding where she made the bride's gown and seven (yes, seven) bridesmaid's gowns. She was up all night for three straight nights before that one, finishing every one with great attention to detail.

When I would wake in the morning, I would ask her if she had slept at all. "I took a couple of twenty minute naps," was always her response. She would set the timer on the stove and when the twenty minutes was up, so was she. It always amazed me how she could do that. It seemed every "nap" I took lasted at least 2 hours!

When we arrived home on Monday morning, Cheryl immediately began preparing for work. I let her go ahead, because my job did not require specific hours, although, at times, it was not uncommon for me to put in 70-80 hours per week. When she was dressed and off to school, I showered, dressed and headed to my office. As I approached the long drive up to the school, I said another prayer that went something like this, "*Lord, right now I want to pause and thank you for putting me in this place, in this job, surrounded by these people. They are a blessing to me and I thank you for each one. Allow me to be your instrument today.*"

I parked my truck in my usual space and walked slowly into the building. The birds were unbelievably loud—louder than I'd ever noticed. Maybe it was just that I noticed them more this morning. I swiped my fob and walked in the building. The secretary's desk faces the main entrance and as I entered, both secretaries looked up through the large glass walls that separate the office from the main hallway. Large smiles appeared on their faces. Joyce and Linda had been secretaries at the school for many years. When I was hired, Linda was the first non-administrator I met. She was the Athletic Secretary and worked on attendance and had a variety of other responsibilities. Joyce worked for the administrators that were in the office, but the two of them worked very well together to keep the place running smoothly. I often talked to them about how it's the secretaries and custodians that run the school, not the administrators, and we always had a good chuckle about that.

"Hello Randy, how are you doing?" they both said, almost in unison.

"I'm doing well. How are things going around here?"

"We are doing just fine," was Joyce's response.

Linda showed a real sense of compassion as she asked, "How are things with your mother?"

I began to describe my last four days and all the things that we had both been through. In the meantime, our Middle School principal Dennis, and our High School principal Brad, heard my voice and joined us. It took me a few minutes to fill them all in, as well as apologizing for not keeping them more updated.

After a few questions regarding a range of topics, I unlocked my office, then went around the corner and entered Brad's office so he could bring me up to date on any pertinent information regarding the athletic department. There really wasn't much going on right then, so things had gone smoothly enough. I told him I would probably be out the rest of the week, but that I wanted to get everything ready that was needed for the following week when Spring sports started. I had a busy day in front of me. He assured me that would be fine, and asked if I had talked to my assistant, Lisa, yet. I told him it was on my list of things to get done before I left today. I left his office feeling like I had his full support. That was important to me.

I settled into my office to try to catch up and prepare for the coming week. I listened to my messages, and two of them struck me particularly hard. They were both from other Athletic Directors in our conference. The first was from Ryan. He had been hired at his school the same time I was hired at mine. We often leaned heavily on each other for advice about work and our personal lives.

"Randy, this is Ryan. Hey, I heard about your Mother's accident. Hope she's doing better. Just wanted to let you know that if you need anything, you've got my cell number, give me a call. I'm not sure if you have baseball and softball games Saturday or early next week, but if you need help with getting fields set up or officials or anything, let me know. It wouldn't take me long to get there. Good luck and keep in touch."

What a good man, and a good friend.

The other came from another Athletic Director in our conference. I had known John for nearly twenty years and we had gotten to know each other very well. John and I had interviewed for the same job that he currently has.

"Randy, this is John. Wanted to let you know that if you need anything, let me know. I will help wherever I can. I will say a prayer for you and your mother at church today, when I go. You have my number, don't hesitate to call if you need something."

I stopped and prayed again. "*Thanks Lord, for bringing these two guys along to help me. They are good friends and people I can count on.*"

When the bell rang for class change, I walked down to Geoff's classroom to thank him for taking care of the starter shells errand and to make sure all went well. He assured me it did and that everything was fine. We briefly discussed Mom's situation and then I left him so he could start class.

My faculty manager, Lisa, was an incredible blessing during this time. No sooner had I sat down in my office, than she appeared at my door. She had tears in her eyes as she entered. I'm not a big one for showing emotion or hugs or that sort of thing in the workplace, but her heart seemed to be breaking. She gave me a hug and asked how things were going. We chatted about the wreck a little while.

"Well, Mom is holding her own, for now. We've got a long road ahead of us, and it will be difficult. If God wills her to live, we will move forward. If God needs her more than we do, then we will deal with that when it comes."

"I don't know how you can be so strong," she replied.

"The power of my Lord gives me all the strength I need. It's in His hands, and no matter how much I'd like to be in charge, I'm not. He is." The words were meant as much for me as for her.

"I hurt so badly for you. Please tell me how you are doing." We closed the door and I proceeded to fill her in. We also talked about how I may need to lean on her a little more in the coming days and maybe even weeks to get us through the spring sports season.

"I can do anything you need," she said. I knew she could. This was our third year working together and she knew how I wanted everything done. She was an incredible asset to me and to Cheryl. Lisa took on a great deal of responsibility that allowed me a few extra precious hours at home with my wife. Cheryl appreciated her so much too.

As she left, she forced a smile onto her face, hugged me again, and said, "We will be praying for you and your mother. I'll take care of things here. You take care of your family."

Lisa left feeling better than before, and as she did, I prayed, "*Lord, quiet her heart. Give her the strength and knowledge to be able to handle the things that come up.*"

After returning a few phone calls and taking care of the officials pay slips, and a few other odd jobs, the bell had rung for class change, and our Head Boys' Basketball coach came in. He too, was a great man of God. We had several conversations over the years about how sports and living a Christian life were related. I trusted him implicitly with every detail of my job, and trusted him that our conversations were always held in the strictest confidence. Tom was truly a bright light in the community and an excellent role model for our kids.

When he came in, he shook my hand, closed the door and sat down.

"Been kind of a tough week for you, hasn't it?" he inquired.

"Yes it has, but God's in charge, so I'm fine," I replied.

"How is your mother doing?"

I proceeded to explain everything again to my new audience, and when I had finished, Tom just answered with, "Wow!"

"Do you have anything you need help with for baseball or softball?" he asked.

Tom served as our JV baseball coach, so I inquired as to whether he could ensure that the officials for JV baseball and softball games got paid. Lisa had said she would do it, but her two daughters both played Varsity softball, and this would allow her to get to the away games easier. Tom agreed he would. He left my office with a handshake and a kind word.

I settled back in to my paper work. There were a couple of Purchase Orders that had to be completed before I left for the day, so I finished those, got Brad to sign them and then set off to the Board Office which was located a short distance across the street from our building. I met several employees along the way, and each asked about Mom and received the paraphrased version of the story as I passed. What normally should have taken about 5 minutes to walk, took well over 20. The well-wishers were appreciated though and I made the effort to tell them that. Once I got outside, the sun was warm and the air was fresh. "*Thank you for all of them,*" I said. "*Thanks for putting me in this place, at this time.*"

Tom's wife Nancy, worked in our treasurer's office as a clerk. She was also our cheerleader advisor and a top-quality person. Anytime I went to her office to drop off or pick up paperwork, she was listening to contemporary Christian music. I always liked that about her. When I walked in with my PO's, she welled up with tears in her eyes. She hopped out from behind her desk and gave me a nice hug.

"How are you, and how is your Mom?" she questioned.

I told her things were as good as could be expected at this point, and that I would know more by the time I got back there later that afternoon.

"What happened that caused the accident?"

So, I went through the whole story again. I didn't mind because the care these people were showing was such a blessing. It would have been easier for me if they hadn't all been asking the same questions and I was giving the same answers, but this was a blessing in that they all wanted to be in this part of my life, right now. "Exactly what I need, and exactly when I need it," had become my motto.

"Nancy, could I ask you a favor? When those PO's get issued, can you call the vendors for me and give them the information? I don't know for sure when I will be in again."

She agreed and we exchanged the usual niceties. As I was leaving, she said that she had put Mom and me on the prayer list at her church. I told her that was great. Another blessing that always helps in these situations is the knowledge that fellow believers are praying for you.

By about 2:00, I had taken care of most of the pressing business that needed my attention. I checked in with Brad, Linda and Joyce, and Lisa one more time before I left, telling each one I'd try to be back in sometime near the end of the week to deal with anything that needed my attention. Unfortunately, that didn't happen. As I left that afternoon to return to Toledo, each of my co-workers echoed Lisa's sentiments. God is good.

Cheryl would not be done with her workday until about 3:30, so I took the short detour on my way home that led to her school. After a quick check in at the office and another discussion of Mom's condition, I walked down the hall to Cheryl's room. When I got to her door, her students were sitting quietly doing some seatwork and my lovely bride was sitting at her desk in the back finishing her daily activities. Meanwhile, her co-teacher Jeff was circulating around making sure the students were all on-task and understanding everything they were doing. Jeff is the husband of the Lutheran minister in one of the other towns in which I had worked. Amy had also served as a track coach while I was there, so I actually knew her before I knew him. Since then, we have become very good friends and we try to have dinner at a local restaurant with Jeff and Amy every couple of months or so. They are great people and terrific friends.

Cheryl looked up and saw me standing outside the door and came out to see me.

"I'm going home to pack a few clothes and head back up to Toledo," I told her.

"Ok, be careful driving. I guess I'll see you tomorrow night."

"That will be great. You and Arielle drive safely, please. I'll call you at home tonight when I know how things went today for her. They were supposed to be doing some neurological tests today. Hopefully, they will have some news for me by the time I get back up there. They told me the other day that the doctors do their rounds starting around 5:00 in the evening. I'd like to be there by then."

"You drive safely too. I love you and I'll miss you."

"OK honey, we'll talk tonight. Love you too. Bye."

As I walked down the hall toward the exit, I wondered how things had gone for Mom today. It was the first I had had time to really think. I would soon find out that it wasn't going well for her.

"Lord you promised that you would take my right hand and be with me. Tonight, I am going to need to claim that promise. Hold me and guide me."

CHAPTER 11

"The Lord your God is with you, He is mighty to save. He will take great delight in you, he will quiet you with his love, he will rejoice over you with singing."

— Zephaniah 3:17 (NIV)

The ride to Toledo seemed to go on for an eternity. I had my bag packed with enough clothes for at least the rest of the week. I had figured it would be at least that long until we really knew what was going to happen, both long and short-term. I called Mark and Aunt Janice when I got back on the Turnpike, to give them both an update. I told Mark I'd be at the hospital until at least Friday, and he said he'd take care of the farm. After a couple of questions regarding a couple of the pregnant cows, he was satisfied that everything would go just fine. It was nearing planting season, and our tenant, Steve, would be starting to work the fields soon. I realized that I hadn't told him about Mom, so, once I finished my calls, I dialed his number.

"Hello," was the response on the other end of the line.

"Steve, this is Randy. I don't know if you had heard about Mom's crash or not. But I wanted to call you myself and fill you in if you have a minute."

"Sure, I've got time. Yea, I had heard through the grapevine, that she was in an accident. How's she doing?"

After apologizing for not calling him sooner, I explained what I knew and let him know I would be in Toledo the rest of the week. He could call me whenever he wanted to, or contact Mark.

"OK, will do," was Steve's reply, "Be careful. Good bye."

The rest of the trip was quiet. I drove on through the rain that was falling and thought that it was a little depressing. This was really my first real shot of melancholy since the whole ordeal began. Sadness gripped me as I pulled into the parking lot, grabbed my bag and headed toward my "Home Away From Home". It was good to be here and not on the road, at least for now.

"Lord, I don't know what is going to happen tonight or tomorrow or the next day. The only thing I am sure of is that you are in charge and whatever you want will be done. Give me the strength to understand that and to have peace with your plan. Thank you Lord, for handling all of this. I can't do this by myself."

It seemed like I was praying constantly, and was always saying the same things. But it was all I could think of and all I needed to say. I was so lucky to have Him guiding and protecting me as I traveled along this path. I'm really not sure how people who don't believe in Jesus Christ as their personal Lord and Savior ever manage their way through situations like this. I know they come out the other side, but maybe the bitterness or resentment or hatred they feel is because they don't rely on the only One that is really running the show. Maybe that was my epiphany in all of this. Because there was nothing I could have done to prevent it, because there was nothing I could do to make it better, because I had no control of what would happen next, I *had* to turn it over to Him. What choice did I have?

As I entered the ICU ward, I was glad to see a familiar face. The nurse from the first day Mom was there was now sitting behind the desk. She looked up from her work and smiled at me. I was glad she was on duty.

"Hello, Mr. Hord," she said.

"Good evening, how are you tonight, kiddo?" I responded. I use that term to provide the person to whom I am talking a sense of warmth and acceptance. I've used it for many years with my students and to acknowledge others with whom I come into contact.

I glanced into Mom's room and saw nothing had changed, at least on the outside.

"How did things go today?" I inquired.

"Let's go in her room and we'll talk about it."

As we talked softly, Nurse J told me she had done all right today, but that her urine output was down a bit from the previous day. "In and of itself, it's not terribly significant, except that if it is a trend over several hours or days, it could indicate the kidneys are starting to shut down."

This was the first indication, as far as I knew, that things were starting to take a turn for the worse.

"Any other problems?" I must have looked a little shaken.

"Nothing else right now. The doctors had asked me to let them know when you got here. They'd like to discuss her progress with you. I'll let them know you are here."

"Thank you." It was about all I could muster at that point. I had noticed the depth of the nurse's eyes as she talked to me. It hurt her to have to give me such news. She had a deep sense of caring for, not only Mom, but Deb and I as well, and our entire family, too. We were fortunate that God had put us and her in this place.

Too many times I think we believe that for Health Care workers, life and death are all too mundane. They see it all the time, so why wouldn't they become somewhat cavalier about it after a while? This could not be farther from the truth. All of them honor life and ache with death. This could not have been any more evident than what we would witness at St. Vincent's over the next 48-72 hours. What an incredibly wonderful, thoughtful and caring staff they have and there was never a moment where Mom, or our family, was treated casually. They really cared for everyone involved and it was very evident. They certainly were filled with God's grace and mercy.

I slumped down in the chair near Mom's bed to just think, project, and reminisce. It was my time with her. I had a feeling she sensed she was slipping, but wasn't quite ready to give up yet. We weren't done, and as long as she wanted to fight, we'd fight together.

Totally lost in my thoughts, I barely noticed when the neurology intern appeared at the large sliding glass door that separated Mom's room from the rest of the ICU.

"Hello, Mr. Hord," she said. "How are you today?"

"As good as can be expected, I guess."

"Let's have a little talk about your mother's progress and prognosis, shall we?"

"I'd like that," I said.

She proceeded to fill me in on the tests they had performed that day. The blood work showed a couple of anomalies that indicated there were some organs beginning to slow their functions. She reiterated the point the nurse had made regarding the urine output. There had been a small response to pain when checked around noon. She showed me how they had done that check. Doctor K removed a pen from the pocket of her lab coat and holding it against one of Mom's toenails, squeezed rather hard. She explained that even a comatose patient will show some reaction, most of the time, to this test. Mom's left hand moved slightly and a quick movement of her eyebrow indicated she might have had some feeling there. That seemed to be a good sign to me.

"Please don't read a lot into that, but it shows there are still some pain sensations there."

I asked the doctor what the prognosis was. She said that the next 24 hours were crucial. We needed to see some improvement in brain waves and that the urine production needed to increase and clear up. The dark yellow, almost brown, was not a good sign.

A little shocked, I asked her if this was the beginning of the end for my mother. The doctor said they weren't ready to say that quite yet, but Mom would need to make a turnaround soon to prevent further damage to her internal organs. Her heart was still strong, but her brain waves were becoming more and more erratic and these were a big concern right now. Her brain was still swelling and that was putting pressure on key points of the brain responsible for many of the bodily functions. Then she finished with a statement that really hit me hard.

"If we don't see a change for the positive soon, we may need to be thinking about how long we keep her attached to the machines." She said it in the kindest, most loving way possible, but it was still quite a blow. I hadn't really thought about it much.

"When will we need that decision to be made?" I questioned.

"We have a little time, but I wanted you to be thinking about all the alternatives and possibilities. I'm sorry I had to bring it up now, but it's something that needed to be said."

She excused herself and left. Wow, that was a shot! Mom might well be dying.

Somehow, my thoughts went back to the gentleman that hit her. How difficult would this be for him? How might this affect his family? I couldn't imagine what he must have been going through. A pang of sadness swept over me. "*Lord, be with him*," I said out loud.

It was prayer time again. I prayed first, for the doctor and her job. How many times had she had to tell other families the same things she had just said to me? I prayed for her peace of mind. Then I prayed for Mom. I prayed that God would work His will in her life. If He needed her to come home now, more than we needed her, then He should take her on His timing. I knew at the time that He didn't need my permission, but I believe that often prayer, when done properly is simply our chance to talk to God for our own needs. That was what that prayer was all about. Then I prayed for Mom's family. I knew it would be hard for her brothers and sisters to let her go. I prayed they would have peace also. I prayed for Deb and Mike, Rachel and Noel, Arielle and Cheryl. They were all very close to Mom and loved her dearly. No matter what, it would hit them very hard when I broke this to them.

The rest of Monday was difficult, but even at that, Mom seemed to be holding on. At times, the nurse would come in and say something like, "Well, that is an improvement," referring to one of the vital signs she had just checked. Then at other times, she'd not say anything at all, which to me meant that it either had not improved or was slowly getting worse.

I remember that it was a strange Monday night because no one came to visit. Sometimes I think I needed the visitors as much as they needed to see Mom. It was a challenging time. I sat and just let my mind wander. I thought about Mom and Dad finally being together in Glory. I was sure they would rejoice and dance and talk and laugh. They were always involved in Square Dancing and I could see them having a big hootenanny when she arrived. Mom had been quite sad the last couple of years since Dad had been gone. She tried not to show it much, but I could tell that she missed the man whom she had known and loved for over fifty years. She enjoyed telling stories about their initial meetings and how much she despised him because of his shenanigans. He was, by all accounts, a real rascal. That is the part he passed on to me. She often commented that I was just like him. That was scary to everyone who knew both of us.

She was dating Dad's best friend, Lyndel, at the time they met. Lyndel convinced Dad to double date with another female friend of theirs. I guess Dad was so obnoxious and ornery that, at the end of the night, Mom told her date she never wanted to ever see him again. That was not in God's plan. Soon after, Mom and her "beau" decided to "break up" and Dad asked her out. Many, many, many requests later she gave in and went out with him. I think it was more so she could tell him she didn't want to go out anymore than anything. It turned out they had a very nice time. "He was on his best behavior that night," she would tell me later. The rest, as they say, is history.

I smiled and enjoyed those memories. What a blessing it was to recall her stories. She spent a lot of time when we were kids talking to us and telling us family anecdotes. Most were of her time growing up, or what she knew of Dad's childhood. She often mentioned relatives on both sides that I didn't know, but it didn't matter. She could really "spin a yarn". The first time she used that term, I had no idea what she meant. When I asked her, she said that was the term my maternal great-grandfather used to say that meant someone was a good storyteller. I smiled again.

Suddenly, there in the quiet of the ICU, I was struck with a deep sadness. We were nearing the end. Mom may not make it through all this. She would probably not go back to the farm. The thoughts washed over me like a flood. I started to feel tears welling up in my eyes. They stung as though someone had thrown a cup of onion juice in my eyes. The burning wouldn't stop. Finally, the tears exploded and trailed down my cheeks and dripped onto my lap. I couldn't help it, and I couldn't stop it. I got up and went to the stand near the sink in Mom's hospital room and grabbed a tissue or two. I wiped my eyes and rubbed the sniffles from my nose. I could not believe I had broken down so completely.

"This is not like me," I thought. "I'm tougher than this. Suck it up and be a man."

But the hurt was too strong. I no longer cared about presenting a tough exterior. There was no one else here for whom I needed to be strong. It was my Mother and I and no one else. I walked to the door and softly asked the nurse if it would be all right if I pulled it shut a little ways. She looked up and saw my face.

"Sure, go ahead, what ever you need."

I pulled the door nearly closed, leaving it open a few inches. I just needed some private time. I believe I had filled my time on purpose so I didn't have to think. Now, with no one else around, I did think, and it hurt. Mom was probably not going home to the farm, but she would be going home—to her Lord and Father. Oh what a glorious time that would be. Jesus would be standing there with His arms wide open welcoming her to heaven. I cried even harder.

The words of Zephaniah 3 came back to me. God was in control. He and his angels were singing over her. They were singing over me too.

CHAPTER 12

"I am the Alpha and Omega," says the Lord
God, "who is, and who was and who is to come,
the Almighty."

– Revelation 1:8 (NIV)

By about 9:00 I had recovered from my fit of gloominess and decided to take a walk. I excused myself with the nurse and walked to the cafeteria. As I stood there looking at the food, I realized that, other than some fruit I had eaten earlier in the day, I had not had anything else all day. I grabbed a pre-made sandwich, some milk, and a bottle of water. I walked to the cashier and paid her using the money Dick had handed me earlier. I smiled thinking about his sadness in all of this too. I wouldn't say that my Mother and Father-in-law were close, but after Dad was gone and Blanche, Cheryl's stepmother passed away, Dick often asked how Mom was doing. In fact, it had gotten to the point where he helped me around the farm so much, that I gave him a key to the shop. He was very proud of that. He had farmed for many years, and although the term was not in use at the time, the shop on his farm was his "Man Cave". He had a couch, a refrigerator that always had a couple of beers in it, and besides his tools, one could always find a radio or old stereo system or some form of entertainment usually tuned to the local country station.

Even though Dick did not attend church regularly, and I'm not sure whether he was Christian or not, I always had a lot of respect for my father-in-law. He was a good, hard-working man that cared deeply about his three daughters. Any tragedy they suffered, he suffered with them. He was devastated when his youngest daughter, Rhonda, lost her husband to a heart attack at 33. He was very upset when his oldest daughter got a divorce, and now, it was very evident that he was really concerned for Mom's welfare. Ironically, while I was eating, and while I was thinking about him, he called to check on her.

"Hello," I answered.

"Randy, how's your mother?" was the gruff voice from the other end.

I explained what had happened during the day and that it was starting to look worse for her.

"Are you alone?"

"Yes, Cheryl and Arielle are coming up tomorrow night to spend the night with me. I did get one of the rooms in the 'Home Away From Home' area that I was telling you about. They are really nice and I think I'll sleep well there."

"Do you want me to come up and stay with you?" I almost laughed out loud.

"No Sir. It's late and I'll be all right for now. I'm eating now, then I'll check back in with her and go to my room and turn in for the night."

"OK, well let me know if you need anything. Have you got money?" This was always his question.

"Yea, I'm fine. Thanks. I'll talk to you later. Thanks for calling."

"Ok." He hung up. He never was much for "Good bye".

I called Deb and updated her with some information, but not all of it. She didn't need, at that point to be worried about anything. I asked her if she was going to be able to come up on Tuesday. She said she would come after work. I told her to see if she could take the day off on Wednesday to be here. She said she'd try, and our conversation ended with that.

I went back to Mom's room, chatted briefly with the nurse, and headed off to my room for the night. I had brought a book and my Bible back with me from home. I pulled them out of my luggage and sat in the recliner near the window to read. I looked out over the city and wondered how many had loved ones that were hurting, either physically, like Mom, or emotionally or mentally. Did they have the promises of an all-powerful Father to lean on like I did? I wished it for all of them. I am truly blessed by the Almighty God that is so omnipresent and omniscient that I have nothing to worry about. Revelation 1:8 came to my mind. I opened my Bible and read the words that summarized this whole experience.

"I am the Alpha and Omega," says the Lord God, "who is, and who was and who is to come, the Almighty."

I called Cheryl to say goodnight. We chatted for a bit about what had transpired during the day and my premonitions about the future.

"I don't think this is going to end with Mom going back to the farm," I told Cheryl.

"It sounds like things took a turn for the worse, huh? Well, it's in God's hands you know. Try to sleep well tonight and I will see you tomorrow night when Arielle and I get there."

"You guys be careful driving and I'll see you when you get here. Love you, honey. I thank God for you a hundred times a day."

"I love you too, Dear," was her response. "Good night. Sleep well. See you tomorrow."

"OK, honey. Good night."

A quick prayer was in order before I fell asleep.

"Thank you Lord for all you are doing and for all your workings and for your plan. I place Mom in your loving arms. Hold her tight and keep her by Your side. She belongs to you. Do with her according to Your will."

I drifted off to sleep around 11:00 and I actually slept very well. God was in control. Why wouldn't I?

CHAPTER 13

*"Come to Me, all you who are weary and
burdened, and I will give you rest…for I am
gentle and humble in heart and you will find
rest for your souls."*

– Matthew 12:28-29b (NIV)

Tuesday was a dull and dreary day outside, but I awoke very
refreshed and ready for whatever God brought my way. It was just
after 6 AM when I walked into the ICU. As I approached Mom's
room there was a bustle of activity. A couple of nurses and orderlies
were huddled around the bed.

"Good morning," I said.

"Good morning, Mr. Hord. How did you sleep?" the night nurse
replied as she approached me.

"We are cleaning up your mother's bed. Her bowels are very loose
and it made quite a mess. Why don't you go get some breakfast and
by the time you get back, we'll have her all cleaned up."

I told her I thought that was a very good idea. After inquiring if a
half-hour would be long enough, and being assured that it would,
I set off for the cafeteria.

The cafeteria was abuzz with activity. Doctors, nurses, orderlies and all sorts of people were scampering about, each with their selections, before they headed off for their daily activities. Even though I was a little concerned about Mom and what, if anything, this most recent occurrence meant, I chuckled inside at how much it reminded me of the anthill just outside King's enclosure.

At times, when he didn't know I was around, I would see the dog playing and barking at the ants as they scurried around doing what it is that ants do all day. He would playfully hop, landing with both front feet on an ant. The great hunter had captured his prey, only to find that 100 others were right next to him going about their business. He would then choose one of them, hunker down on his rear haunches, wiggle his rear, bark and then repeat the hopping motion. It always made me laugh. King was a good dog and a joy for Mom. I wondered how he was getting along at Uncle Ben and Aunt Miriam's house.

King's story shows how God blesses us by taking care of all the details when we just trust Him to do so. After the crash, Uncle Ben asked if he should get the dog and take him to their home. I thanked him and assured him that would be a great idea. The kennel where Mom boarded King when she took her vacations is located less than two miles from their house. The husband and wife that run the kennel are people our family has known for many years. The gentleman was in my sister's class in high school and was one of my football teammates. They contacted Aunt Miriam two days after the crash and offered to board King for free for as long as we needed it. Praise God for that offer. Aunt Miriam politely thanked them and declined the offer telling those incredible people King would stay with them until all got settled with Mom. Another blessing came raining down. Thank you Lord.

After I got what I wanted for breakfast, I went to a nearby table and sat down. "I should call Mark and Aunt Janice," I thought to myself, "but I think I'll wait until I have more information." Just then the phone rang. It was Cheryl. The line from the old country song, "The first thing every morning and the last thing every night," came to mind.

"Good morning honey," she replied in the most chipper voice she could muster. "How are you this morning?"

"I'm OK."

"You don't sound so good, didn't you sleep well?"

"I actually slept pretty well. I'm just concerned about Mom. They had a mess in her bed this morning. Her bowels aren't functioning very well."

"She hasn't had any solid food in several days. Don't put too much stock in that until you talk to one of the doctors," she said in the most loving tone imaginable.

I really missed her. We hadn't spent many nights apart since we were married over thirty years before. I occasionally would go to a coaches' clinic out of town for a night or two, but even that didn't feel right. I missed her so much right then.

"Yea, you are probably right," I responded. "I will just wait until I get to talk to someone."

We spent the rest of the conversation discussing her day and that Arielle was coming home and we would all be reunited tonight. It was a nice chat, but it was time for Cheryl to get ready for school. We said our goodbyes and she hung up. I finished my breakfast and walked slowly toward the elevators. I could feel the burden of the upcoming decision weighing on my shoulders. I wasn't excited to make that decision. I think I already knew what was going to have to be done.

I knew in my head that God would make this easier to do, but my heart hadn't gotten the complete message yet. I wanted to trust Him, I was trying to trust Him, but sometimes the carnal man in me kept fighting back. It kept telling me I should be angry, upset, hateful, and all sorts of other negative emotions toward everyone and everything around me. "Look at the work you are missing. Look at your Mother; she's in a coma. Look at all the things that man did to you when he caused the wreck." I knew that those were all wrong, that they didn't belong in my thoughts, but they were there. Amazingly, just as these thoughts were going through my mind, I walked right past the chapel. Praise God! I went in and sat down. Now it was just God and I and my terrible thoughts. I started with a prayer.

God, I need you now. I need Your peace. I need to be able to understand Your plan and what You want me to do. I can't do this alone. I don't want to feel bitterness or hatred. I want to be focused on You and what You are doing for Your glory. I know this is what you have asked of us, of me, and it's what I want to do. But my God, it is so hard. I am weak and Thou art strong. Fill me with Your strength. Please Lord help me.

The answer flashed into my mind immediately from Matthew 28:20b, which says, "...*surely I am with you always, to the very end of the earth.*" Followed closely after that came a passage from Isaiah 41:15. "*So do not fear, for I am with you; do not be dismayed for I am your God. I will strengthen you and help you; I will uphold you with my righteous right hand.*"

I have come to really appreciate the NIV translation. To me, it is easier to read and understand than the other translations. It's more like I'm praying, in my language, when I read it. At that point, I was secretly thanking all those Sunday School teachers that made me attempt to memorize all those scriptures. The challenge for them was to convince this wayward son that someday I would need these scriptures in my "real" life. I remembered enough to be useful now. It was all I needed, and exactly when I needed it. Praise the Lord.

I finished my meditation with another short prayer and moved out the door and toward the elevator. I wiped away the tears and sniffles. There, standing in front of the elevator, was Lanny. Wow God, you did it again!

"Hi Randy. How are you doing?"

"I'm doing OK, Lanny. It's good to see you again."

"How are things going with your Mother?" His simple question brought deep sadness to my heart. It was not intentional on his part, he didn't know.

"She has started to take a turn for the worse," I said, just as the elevator arrived. "She is having some problems internally."

"I'm so sorry," he said. "Let's pray."

Again, exactly what I needed, exactly when I needed it, and from a man who had already blessed me so much, came another great blessing.

"Lord, I want to ask for your guiding hand on Randy over the next few days as he deals with the events that you have planned. Help him

to realize it is You who is in charge, it is Your plan and that You have him and his mother in Your hands. Thank you Lord for this man of God and help him to exhibit Your Grace in all he does. Amen."

"Thanks Lanny, I appreciate that."

As we exited the elevator and turned up the hall toward the ICU, we talked softly about a variety of topics. Lanny pushed the large wall button and the doors parted. We greeted the nurse and went into Mom's room.

The first thing I noticed was how ashen my Mother's face and skin looked. It had lost the natural color that I had always been so used to. I commented about it and Lanny nodded. He asked if there was anything he could do. I told him I thought I was all right for now. He asked how my room was. "Great, thank you for making those arrangements for me." Again, Lanny nodded. He offered up a brief prayer for Mom and me and then excused himself. I really appreciated that God had provided that contact with him on such a dull, dreary morning. Lanny is a good man and perfectly designed for his ministry. Praise the Lord for him.

I'm not always convinced that as we go about our calling, we really understand the impact we have on people. We get so used to doing what we do, that often times, I think we forget that to the person receiving our gift, this is a whole new experience for them. The love we show, through our Lord Jesus Christ, is genuine. We don't expect anything in return, and yet, somehow, the person to whom we are ministering needs what we have to offer right then. God puts us there, at that moment, because that is what He has called us to do. Lanny is like that.

Soon after I settled in, the intern, Dr. K, strode into the room. It was nice to see her again. We had connected in our earlier meetings and I felt as though she were a confidant. I appreciated that right now, because I needed someone to talk to.

"Good morning, Mr. Hord."

"Good morning, Doc."

"How are you doing this morning? Did you get any sleep?"

"Actually, I slept pretty well. The 'Home Away From Home' rooms are very nice. I appreciate that St. Vincent's has that available. How are you doing?"

As we were talking, she reached in her lab coat and took out her pen. She turned up the sheet on the end of Mom's bed and pressed the pen across one of the toenails of Mom's right foot. No reaction. She slowly lowered that sheet and retested the left foot. Again, there was no reaction.

"I'm well, thanks for asking. I've taken a look at your mother's charts from the last 24 hours. I believe there are some problems beginning to develop. The blood tests show that there are some toxins beginning to appear in the blood that show that some of her internal organs are in the early stages of shutting down. They aren't critical as of 3 AM this morning, but they are elevated. Have you given any more thought to our discussion of yesterday?"

By now, the ER neurologist, her cooperating doctor had joined us.

"Oh, yes ma'am, I have. I've been doing little else than praying and thinking since then."

"Have you got any family you can call on to help you if you need to make this decision. If you do, you should probably contact them soon."

This reply hit me like a ton of bricks. It sounded now like Mom was already gone. There was no hope. A sense of despair struck my heart so hard I could barely breathe. I searched my memory bank for some solace from God's word. It came to me from Psalm 33:20-22.

"We wait in hope for the Lord; He is our help and our shield. In Him our hearts rejoice, for we trust in His holy name. May Your unfailing love rest upon us, O Lord, even as we put our hope in You."

"My sister will be here this evening after she gets off work," I replied. "I will have to discuss it with her and we will make the final decision together."

"I'm glad you have someone to rely on. That makes these decisions a lot easier to handle." Her voice was soft and her eyes showed deep compassion as she spoke. "We will continue to monitor her, but you should be prepared if we decide that she can't take much more."

I thanked her and shook her hand and Dr. R's too.

"Thank you Lord, for them and their work."

CHAPTER 14

"Peace I leave with you; my peace I give you. I do not give to you as the world gives. Do not let your hearts be troubled and do not be afraid."

– John 14:27 (NIV)

The rest of the day was a blur of lost time as I drifted between my childhood, my family, her family, our church family and the present. The decision that was coming would not be an easy one, but I had a feeling I knew what it was going to be.

As the afternoon wore on, I would occasionally get up from my chair and walk around the room or down the hall and back, but mostly I just sat in Mom's room looking at her and thinking. At one point I got up to walk around her bed and looked at her urine bag. It was nearly brown. "That's not good," I thought to myself. She's regressing. I would listen to her breathing, and sometimes it would be very shallow and faint and sometimes it would be very heavy and labored. That was not a good sign either.

The machines continued their attempts to pump life throughout her tattered body, but it was evident, that, at times, she was not cooperating much. The sounds the machines emitted were supposed to be rhythmic and steady. These were anything but. Some would go out of rhythm or stop beeping at all, while others would whine at a constant pitch for a couple of minutes until the duty nurse came and checked it. By punching a button on one machine or the other, she could reset it for a while. They were so efficient at what they did.

Some time later, Cheryl related a story to me that could only be called miraculous. Around 5:30 that night, as she sat at home waiting for Arielle to arrive from West Virginia, Cheryl was reading from one of her favorite books when she suddenly felt a cool breeze move past her. The windows and doors were all closed, but it was strong enough to ruffle her hair as it went by. She stopped reading and looked around the room. There was nothing around that would have created such a wind.

As she told me this story later, she said, "I believe it was your Mother passing through to say, 'Goodbye.' I really believe at that point was when she actually passed on. I was glad she stopped by to let me know," Cheryl told me with a tear in her eye.

Amazingly, about that same time, Arielle was driving home. She felt her Grandma was with her in her car. These two stories were told to me at two different times without each knowing the other's account. I believe it was Mom's way of saying goodbye to both of them in a very private, very real way. They both were touched so deeply by these events. Mom loved her "girls" and this was her way of letting them know she would be leaving them.

I called Mark and Aunt Linda and gave them some of the information about Mom, trying to be as positive sounding as I could. I wasn't going to lie to them, but I wasn't going to upset anyone either. It was a difficult balance to get that right. If the end were to come, it would be soon enough.

"Mom is holding her own for now," was about all I said.

I had just returned from grabbing a bite to eat in the cafeteria when Deb, Michael and Rachel appeared at the door. It was good to see them. After they all had a chance to talk to Mom, I suggested we go to the Lounge to talk for a while. I wanted to prepare Deb for what was to come, without a lot of people around. We sat down on the large, institutional pastel green couches.

"I think we're going to have some decisions to make soon," I started the conversation. It is said that I'm not real subtle. I don't believe in wasting a lot of time saying what I don't mean.

"Oh really, what do you mean, Randy?" Deb asked. I think she knew what I meant, but she always likes things crystal clear. She doesn't take hints the right way usually.

"Some of Mom's organs have begun to shut down. This afternoon, the toxins in her blood were very high and it seems as though her kidneys and maybe her liver are already headed there. The doctor says the brain waves have also begun to diminish some, although there still seems to be quite a bit of brain activity. Her heart is not totally dependent on the machine, and she is still out-breathing the machine for the most part."

Deb looked very distraught. Her eyes glazed over and tears welled up. As one slowly trickled down her cheek, she reached to the nearby stand and grabbed a tissue.

"We are getting near the end, aren't we?"

"I don't know. I get that feeling, but I just don't know," was all I could think of to say. "The doctors don't believe it is time yet to decide what to do, but they said we should be prepared. There is still enough brain activity that I'm not willing to give up yet, but it doesn't look good."

"Well, we know what her feeling was when Dad was bad. She said to me more than once, she didn't want to be the way he was at the end." Her words simply repeated what Mom had told me several times too. I guess she wanted us to remember it. She always believed in that as an instructional tool—say it often enough and loud enough and people will remember it.

I glanced at Michael and Rachel. Both of them had their heads down and sadness resounded through them. I could read it in each one's body language. They were devastated. Rachel began to cry softly. It was so hard for me to have to say this to them. It would be even harder to repeat it when Cheryl and Arielle got here. I hate this part of the life and death process.

"Mike, could you lead us in a prayer please? I'm almost 'prayed out'."

"Sure, Randy," was his response. His training as a minister and pastoral leader had given him the opportunity to work through these scenarios with other families. Now, he would be able to help us through it too. I really appreciate Mike's way of saying the right things at the right time.

I don't recall the exact words, but they were for strength for Deb and I as we went through the trials of the next few days, for God's will to be done and for safe travel for my family. We just sat there in silence for a few moments after his final "Amen". It was a comforting prayer, something I had not felt for a while. I thanked Mike and asked if we wanted to go back to Mom's room. Rachel and Deb said they would so we sauntered slowly back down the familiar hallway.

When we entered the ICU ward, I could tell that someone was in Mom's room. It was her nurse, a lab technician and Dr. M, the orthopedist.

"Just stopped in to check on Mrs. Hord. I had the nurses replace the bandages on her upper leg and her arms. The wounds are healing, although there is a small amount of redness showing around some of the areas. Her body is trying to fight off infections. I see her urine in very dark and that could be, in part, some blood in the urine from her bruised bladder and kidneys." This was new news to me. These were two more injuries I hadn't heard about. Not that she needed anything else wrong with her. "I will check back in with her after my surgery early tomorrow morning. I should be in around 9:30 or so. Any questions?"

I had thousands, but none seemed appropriate right now. They could all wait.

"No Sir, I don't think so. Deb, you have anything?"

"Nope, not at this point."

"Alright then, I will see you tomorrow." He patted Mom's hand softly before he walked away.

He had seemed more positive from his perspective than the other doctors to which I'd been talking lately. Although the dark urine and the pungent smell that was now becoming more evident by the hour, didn't seem to allay my misgivings about Mom's future.

We just stood there for a while watching Mom sleep until Deb broke the silence.

"He sounded a little more positive," she said trying not to show trepidation in her voice. "Maybe she will recover to some degree." I felt like she said it as much for her sake as for mine.

"We will have to see what happens in the next few hours."

I was trying to be realistic while not being overly pessimistic. Deb needed as much support as possible. I had tried to keep her in the know as much as possible recently, but her family and work responsibilities required her to be at home and it was difficult for her to deal with all the little details that I had processed and she hadn't yet. She had been very supportive over the last few days, and I had tried hard to keep her updated, but I believe the full brunt of the situation was just hitting her now. Deb was sad and no matter what I said at that moment, it wasn't going to make a difference. She needed some space and time to work it all out in her own mind and in her own way. Fortunately, she had her loving husband, daughter and granddaughter to help her. Soon, Cheryl and Arielle would be there too and we would all be together and get through it as a family. The next few hours would not be easy but we were Mom's family. The strength our Mother so amazingly displayed in her life would help us in her death.

My family arrived at the hospital around 11:30 that night. Deb's family greeted them and after a brief discussion with Cheryl and Arielle about the occurrences of the day, Deb, Michael, Rachel and Noel left the hospital to head off to a nearby hotel, promising to return early the next day. We finished a quick chat with Mom's nurse and shuffled off down the hall to the elevator. When we got to the ground floor, we said our goodbyes and they left. We retrieved my family's belongings from Arielle's car and headed toward our room.

"This is really nice," Arielle said looking around our room. "I think I'll take a shower before we go to sleep."

"Sounds like a good idea, honey," her mother replied. "You probably feel a little grungy."

"No kidding." Her reply sounded so much like her Mother that I actually thought it was Cheryl speaking and not Arielle. I grinned to myself a little smile. "Two peas in a pod," I thought.

While Arielle showered, Cheryl and I talked further about the day's events. It was not easy to realize that my Mother was, literally, on her deathbed. Every indication was that she was not going to get better and that she was never going home to the farm.

"We don't have much time with her anymore," I lamented. My loving wife squeezed my hand as we sat on the edge of the bed together. "I don't think she'll be with us much longer. Deb and I have a major decision to make tomorrow."

"Have you talked to her family lately?"

"No, I called Aunt Miriam this morning and told her things were not going as well as before, but I haven't called at all during the day." There really was no new information to give them. She was slowly regressing, and there wasn't much the hospital staff, or we, or her family could do for her.

After Arielle finished her shower, we got ready for bed. Cheryl and Arielle slept on the bed and I slept in the large recliner near the window. I turned it around and faced them so it didn't seem like I was alone. I wasn't, I had my family, and my Heavenly Father with me. I didn't need any more.

"Lord, tomorrow will be in Your hands. Help us to help Mom according to Your plan and Your will. I can't do this alone. I can't do this even with the wonderful family You have placed around me. Give Deb peace and clarity of mind. Work in her heart to calm her. She deserves it Lord. Thank you for her family. Michael is her rock and Rachel and Noel keep her grounded. They are exactly what she needs right now. Thank you for putting us in this place, at this time, with these people. You are strong and I am weak. Help me maintain my dignity, the dignity of our family and especially Mom's dignity throughout what is going to happen tomorrow. Thank you Lord for Your many gifts to us. Amen."

God was in control. I had finally figured that out. It was time to let Him do His work, and not worry about it anymore. I began to feel the same tranquility in my heart that Mom had felt about Dad when he passed away. I was starting to understand how she was so calm and at peace with his passing. She was smart enough to realize it was God that was in charge and He was going to do what He was going to do and there was nothing we could do about it. I had learned her lesson as she was fading away from us. "Love ya, Mom." With that, I drifted off to sleep.

CHAPTER 15

"Fight the good fight of the faith. Take hold of the eternal life to which you were called when you made your confession in the presence of many witnesses. In the sight of God, who gives life to everything, and of Christ Jesus…"

– I Timothy 6:12-13a (NIV)

I awoke to a bright sunshine-filled morning. It was 6:15 AM and time for me to get going. I had slept surprisingly well and as I walked toward the bathroom to take my shower, my wife and daughter both rolled over in bed.

"You OK?" Cheryl asked.

"Yep, I'm fine. I'm going to shower and head over to ICU to see how things went. Let Arielle sleep, she was so tired last night. When you get ready, you can come on over," I said softly so as not to rouse my sleeping beauty from her slumber. I had always enjoyed watching our daughter sleep from the time we brought her home from the hospital. She always slept peacefully and looked so beautiful. This was no exception.

I showered, dressed, kissed Cheryl and moved out the door and across the commons area toward the hallway that led back to the hospital. A small child was busy playing with some toys on the floor as his mother prepared some coffee nearby in the kitchen area. He ran his trucks back and forth on the carpet as he made engine noises with his mouth. The bright sun felt warm as it bounced off the pastel walls of the play area.

"Beautiful day isn't it?" I asked the Mother.

"Yes it is. The sun looks so nice in the mornings." I thought of Mom's love of the mornings and how lucky I was to have had her instill that in me.

"Have a good day," I said to her as I passed through the large glass door.

"You too," was her response.

"Lord, be with them today. I don't know why they are here, but bless that mother and guide her. Wrap Your loving arms around her and let her know You've got her in your care."

It just seemed right to pray for her just then.

I had a choice to walk through the hallway to the hospital, or across the small parking lot, and past the healing garden. I chose the latter. It seemed appropriate to go that way since it seemed to be so nice outside. I was right. It was glorious! The sun was incredibly warm for the second-last day of March. I believe every bird in Toledo had roosted in the trees and bushes nearby just to sing for me. What a blessing that was!

"Here we go again," I thought. "God is going to bless us in even more ways. I can just feel it."

I paused for a couple of moments in the garden to just enjoy where I was and what I was doing. I knew, in the back of my mind, it was going to be a difficult day. But, as I was trying to convince myself, God is good and He is in charge. The passage from Proverbs 3:5-6 came to my mind as I paused there.

"Trust in the Lord with all your heart and lean not on your own understanding; in all your ways submit to him and he will make your paths straight."

It was amazing to me, and still is, that each time something happened or each time I needed a verse, all these thoughts came rushing into my mind. The Spirit was providing me with exactly what I needed, exactly when I needed it, and in exactly the right quantity. I didn't realize until then how much scripture I had learned through the years. It was wonderful to know that the Almighty was leading me, and that he had the whole situation under control. All I had to do was have the faith of "a grain of mustard seed" and He would move my mountain. The mountain lay ahead of us. All we had to do was have faith, and God would handle the rest.

I walked inside, approached the elevator and there waiting next to it was an elderly couple. He was in a wheel chair and she was pushing him. I wondered if they were there to visit someone or if he was coming in as a patient. I asked if I could help and she thanked me as I helped push him into the open elevator door.

"Which floor?" I asked, and as she told me "Three, please", I punched the button for it and then for my floor.

"It is a beautiful day today, isn't it?" I queried.

"It's lovely," she answered.

I got the feeling she really was more concerned about the man in the wheel chair than talking to me. We didn't speak anymore until the doors parted for their floor.

"Have a good day," I said.

"You too, and thank you again."

"Lord, give them a good day. Bless them in ways they can't imagine, just as you have done for me."

The doors closed, the elevator shook as it continued its ascent, and then shook again as it stopped at my floor. I made the short walk towards the ICU, not particularly excited to get there. I had no idea what a long day it was going to be.

There was no one in Mom's room when I arrived just before 7:00, except her and all the machines as they continued their incessant beeping, buzzing and moaning. It seemed to me there ought to have been a way to make a quieter machine for sick peoples' rooms. I smiled at the thought.

I walked over to my Mother's bedside. Her eyes were even more sunken than they had been the night before when we left. I touched her hand. It was cold and lifeless. As I looked back at her face, I spoke.

"Mom, it's Randy. I hope you can hear me. I want you to know how much I love you and that I know I wasn't the easiest son to raise. I put you and Dad through a lot when I was younger and created a lot of heartache for both of you. I'm sorry about that and want you to know that I really do appreciate the man I've become because of who you and Dad were. We spent a lot of time together as a family and I know you guys sacrificed a lot to make that happen. I know how hard your life was and how much it meant to you to provide for Deb and I. I hope someday, I can be half the parent you were. I love you Mom. I always will."

I nodded my head and just stood. No particular thoughts were going through my head. I just stood. I think my heart was preparing me for the day. I know I felt God's presence there, right at that moment.

"Mr. Hord?" It was Mom's nurse.

"Yes."

"Your Mother has not shown much change since last night. Her vitals are about the same, but her blood pressure dropped very low a couple of times last night. The doctors asked that I call them when you arrived. Would you like me to do that now?"

"I'd like my sister to be here when they come in. Let me give her a call. She staying in a nearby hotel, so I will see when she will be here."

"That will be fine, just let me know."

"Thank you."

I left the ICU ward and headed toward the Lounge. I thought that would be a good place to make the necessary phone calls I needed to make.

I started with Cheryl. She said they would be over in a few minutes.

I called Deb. They were all about ready, but it would be a few minutes until they left. I told her the doctors wanted to talk to us and that she should try to get there as soon as possible. We decided that an hour would probably be long enough.

When I returned to the ICU, I relayed that information to the nurse and she contacted the doctors. A short while later, Nurse L came in to check the machines and said the doctors would be there as we discussed. I felt a twinge of sadness. I had a good idea what they were going to say. Only time would tell, but at least we would all be together when the news came.

When the neurologist arrived, closely followed by Dr. K, his intern, I could tell by their body language they didn't have good news to share. Deb and her family arrived soon after and we all stood to one side of Mom's room and discussed the situation.

"Your Mother's internal organs have nearly all shut down. There is almost no brain wave activity, only the very minimal 'primitive' functions. Those are the ones that maintain the breathing and heart. Virtually none of her other brain functions have appeared for several hours."

I heard Deb take a deep breath. Her mother was dying and there was nothing more we could do about it. I felt a pang of sadness for her and put my arm around her. I heard a small sniffle. That was Cheryl, followed by another from Arielle.

The doctor continued. "It is time to consider taking her off the machines. There is virtually no chance that, given her condition now, she will recover. There has just been too much trauma."

"When do we need to decide?" I asked.

"You should go somewhere quiet, sit down and talk about it, and let the nurse know what you've decided. She will contact us, then Palliative Care if that is what you decide. They will help you through the process." Dr. K, the intern, had a profound look of sadness on her face. "Your Mother has fought a good fight, but it is nearly over now."

"Thank you for all you've done. We are thankful for you and all the folks here at the hospital. We will let you know soon." It was all I could think of to say.

Both Doctors shook our hands and excused themselves.

CHAPTER 16

*"Peace I leave with you; my peace I give you. I
do not give to you as the world gives. Do not let
your hearts be troubled and do not be afraid…
If you loved me, you would be glad that I am
going to the Father"*

– John 14: 27 & 28b (NIV)

We all stopped by Mom's bed then walked slowly down the hall to
the Lounge. As we sat down, we all just took a minute to gather
ourselves. I prayed a silent prayer.

*"Lord, I thank you for this place. I thank you for the people that have
worked so hard and with such great care for Mom's sake. I thank you
for my family and their ability to steadfastly hold on to You and Your
will in this journey. Please Lord, give us the understanding now to
first, know Your will, second, to accept Your will and third, to do as
You wish for us to do. Lord, I also pray for the man's family who hit
her. Give them Your presence so they can deal with their emotions in
all of this too. Thank you for what you have done and how you have
worked in all of this. In His name I pray, Amen."*

I broke the silence with, "Deb, what are you thinking right now?"

After a short silence she said, "That's not my Mommy in there, any more." This was the first time in years I had heard her use "Mommy" when referring to our Mother. It brought me back to when a decision had to be made about Dad, and she said nearly the same words using "Daddy".

"She is not going home to the farm, if by some miraculous set of events, she would recover. She always told us she didn't want to be kept alive by machines. Right now, that's what is happening. It's not what she would want."

"I agree," I said. "I think it's time to let her go to her heavenly home. I do want as many of her siblings and their families to be here though before we have the machines removed. I think they would like to be part of this. Would you like for me to talk to the nurse and explain things?" I asked Deb.

Through tear-filled eyes, she nodded and said, "Yes. I will go with you though."

As we walked back down the hall toward the ICU, we didn't say much. I put my arm around her and simply said, "Pretty tough, huh?" She just shook her head. It was agonizing seeing her so sad. She and Mom were as close as any Mother and Daughter could be. I often said that Deb was her "favorite", but I didn't believe she had a favorite, just a special bond between them.

We approached the nurses' station and asked the nurse to come in to Mom's room.

"We've decided to let her go," I said.

"I think that is the right decision," she said. There was sadness in her voice, in her face, in her eyes and throughout her whole body. "She must have been a great lady to have raised such a fine family." We both just nodded in agreement and walked towards Mom's bed. "I'll let Palliative Care know."

"We are letting go Mom," I thought. "Thank you for being who you are. We will miss you. Say 'Hi' to Dad for us. Enjoy the beauty of heaven. I hear the sunrises are incredible." It was all in my thoughts, but I know she heard them.

Deb was lost in her thoughts too. I'm sure her thoughts were similar to mine.

"I will go call her brothers and sisters," I told Deb. "We want them to be here if they can be. We will wait until they are all here and have a had a chance to say their goodbyes."

"That's a good idea," was Deb's response.

Arielle and Rachel had both had a feeling that this was coming, but the news hit them like a Mack truck. They both got teary eyed and hugged each other. They had always been great friends besides being cousins. They confide in each other like sisters. They are both only children, so over the years, they've come to rely on one another for peer support. They don't always agree with what the other is doing, but they have always loved each other very deeply. They were relying on that singleness of mind right now.

They asked us how long it would be before we started the process of removing the machines and we assured them it would not be until later in the day. They wanted to take Noel and go to the "Peace Garden" as they called it. The rock garden where Cheryl and I had spent some time together just a few days before was just the place they needed to be. It was going to be good for them to get away, have some time just to be together, tell stories about Grandma, laugh, cry and laugh some more.

As they were leaving the garden, Arielle reached down and picked up a small pink and black stone from the ground and placed it in the pocket of her fleece jacket. This tiny piece of memorabilia would reflect those moments together. She still has it and carries it with her. She has always been one for collecting tangible objects associated with her special memories. Her bedroom is filled with Sandy Alomar Jr. and Grady Sizemore memorabilia, both of whom are her favorite baseball players. This rock would stand to symbolize her last few hours with Grandma. We love her for who she's become, but we love her every bit as much for how she's gotten there. It's hard to find a more loving, joy-filled and incredible young lady than our daughter. But then again, I might be a little bit biased in that assertion.

Arielle says that as she and Rachel talked, so too did Noel. She told stories of what she and Great-grandma did. All the books they read together, all the things King did and how Great-grandma always yelled at him for everything and all the wonderful times she had at Great-grandma's house when she got to stay overnight. I know how much Mom loved those times too. She would tell us her version of the stories the next day or two afterward. The love Noel had for Great-grandma was reciprocated ten fold and then some. They were a terrific couple and loved each other so much.

"Aunt Miriam, this is Randy."

"Well hello, Randy, how are you?" Aunt Miriam's voice reminded me a great deal of my mothers. Not only did they look a lot alike, they even sounded a lot alike. "How's Marilyn?" The question would be so hard to answer.

"Not well. We've made the decision to remove her from life-support and we'd like the family to come to be with her and us when we do. Can you contact Uncle Wayne and Aunt Linda to let them know, please? I'll get hold of Aunt Carol and have her call Uncle Chuck."

There was a short silence on the other end of the call. "Oh, I'm sorry to hear that you've had to make that choice, but I understand. Sure, I will call them. When do you plan to stop the machines?" Her voice broke a little and I could hear that she was in pain.

"We won't be doing anything until you all get here. But it will probably be mid- to late afternoon. We just want you all to be here."

"OK, thanks for including us. I'll contact Wayne and Linda and we'll make the arrangements to get there as soon as possible. Thanks again for letting us know."

"Sure," I said. "See you this afternoon. Goodbye."

"Wow, that was harder than I thought it would be." That was the only thought I had, but even though there was no one else in the room, I realized I had said it out loud.

I dialed the next number.

"Aunt Carol, this is Randy."

"Oh, Hello Randy, how are you doing?" I smiled at the similarity in the greetings between the two sisters.

"Not so good, we've decided to remove the life-support machines from Mom. She hasn't had any response to stimulus at all in over 36 hours now and her organs are shutting down. Her brain waves are no longer producing any appreciable movement on the scanners. We believe it's time to let her go."

Silence again greeted me. "OK, so when do you plan to do this?" Again I smiled, they were more alike and more like Mom than even they would admit.

"We want to wait until all of her brothers and sisters that wish to, can be here to say goodbyes. We don't think we will start the process until mid-afternoon at the earliest. We'd like you to come if you want to."

"Of course I would."

"Could you call Uncle Chuck for me and see if he wants to be here, please? I know Mindy's not well, but he may want to come. Aunt Miriam is calling the others."

"Sure, I will. We will see you soon."

"OK, thanks," I said. "See you then. Goodbye."

All that was left was to make the other calls necessary, but those could wait. For now, this would be family time. Michael and Deb's family, Cheryl and I with Arielle and Mom would be enough. We had each other and the rest could wait. I wanted to just be with these people and no longer worry about all the decisions that needed to be made. The biggest one was made and we would go on from here.

"Lord, I believe that You have had Your holy hand in all of these things. I believe you brought us to this place, at this time. Thank You for the blessings You have given my family and especially me. Grant me the grace to conduct myself as You would have me do, and give me the patience to handle anything that comes my way in the next hours, days, weeks, months and years. Thank You for the wreck, for the time I had with my mother and for putting me in this situation so You could receive the glory. I owe everything I have, every gift, every person, and every blessing to You. Praise Your holy name. In Jesus I pray, Amen."

It felt right. Mom was going to be with her Jesus that she loved so much. She had dedicated nearly her whole life to loving and serving Him. Now, she was going to get to see Him, face-to-face, in Glory. Oh what a happy time that would be for her. There is no greater feeling for the family left behind than to know that their loved one is going to be with the Lord for all eternity. She would be dancing with her Father God in fields of Grace for an audience of One.

CHAPTER 17

"You prepare a table before me...You anoint my head with oil; my cup overflows. Surely goodness and love will follow me all the days of my life and I will dwell in the house of the Lord forever."

– Psalm 23:5a-6 (NIV)

As noon approached, we chatted and reminisced. Deb and Michael alternated with Rachel in caring for Noel. Cheryl and I sat in Mom's room and talked with each one as they came and went. Wherever Rachel was, there too was Arielle. They were a blessing for each other. It was as though the fifteen months that separated them might as well have been fifteen minutes. Rachel was the older but somewhat shorter statured than Arielle. Her Aunt and Uncle were always teasing Arielle for having "blonde" disease. She never intentionally said things to sound "dizzy", just sometimes it came out that way. They were always there to remind her about it. It was a great source of laughter for all of us over the years.

Just after noon, one of the Palliative Care nurses and one of the Chaplains appeared at the door to Mom's ICU room. They were both solemn and respectful as they entered.

"We'd like to discuss the process we use through our Palliative Care Department," the Chaplain said. "Let's go somewhere we can sit and talk. I think the Lounge would be a good place."

"Oh man, I feel like I'm being called to the principal's office," I joked.

"Well, you should know, you had plenty of practice," Deb retorted and we all had a good laugh. I really believe this made the conversation that followed easier for the nurse and chaplain. We were not mourning. We were celebrating. We were celebrating the going home of one of Jesus' own. God's daughter was going to see him in Heaven. We were sorry to lose her here, but overjoyed that she was going to be without pain, sorrow or worry.

"I did have a lot of practice. They had a 'Reserved for Randy' sign on one of the benches in the office," I quipped. We all laughed again.

"Your family seems to really enjoy each other," I remember the Palliative Care nurse commenting after only about three minutes with us. "You are always laughing and teasing one another."

"We have always been this way. We don't know any other way to be," Deb responded.

"Your mother was a great lady. She must have been to have raised such a terrific, loving family." This was not the first time we had heard this comment, and it would not be the last. They were right. She was pretty remarkable.

"Lord, we pray for this family in the home going of their Mother. Bless them as they are with her and we ask for safe travel for any of the other

family members that are making their way here to be with her too. In Jesus' name we pray, Amen"

"*Amen*," we all repeated. The chaplain's prayer was short and to the point.

"Just the way I like them," I thought.

"I'd like to explain to you what will happen," the nurse said. She was a lovely young lady with light brown hair and blonde highlights. Her blue eyes were piercing and compassionate. She spoke softly but authoritatively. It was obvious she had been through this many times in the past.

"When we are finished here," she said, "you will have some time to go back to your Mother's room and say your goodbyes as you see fit. Take your time; there is no rush for anything we do from here on out. We will go at the speed at which you wish to proceed. The timing is all about the family's wishes, not ours. Will there be anyone else joining us?" she inquired.

"I believe most of her siblings will be here. They are coming from a distance so I don't expect any of them much before about 3:00 or so."

My response was designed to build in some time for just the six of us. I had no idea at that moment that the nurse meant exactly what she had said. It was all about our timing. We could move through the stages as slowly as *we* wanted to. We would experience the great dignity with which these people and this hospital conducted their business. It was incredible. It was more than a "business" to them; it was people and people's lives and loved ones' lives. The blessings continued to fall on us. God had placed us in the right place at the right time with the right people around us. He really did know what He was doing. Praise His name.

"Once you have decided you are ready to start," the nurse continued, "we will ask you to leave for a few minutes so we can remove all the tubes and machines from her except the respirator. When that is finished, we will move her to our Palliative Care ward. It is on the same floor as the ICU and right down the hall. I will show you when we are finished here." There was almost a noticeable sadness in her voice.

Michael broke the intensity with one of his one-liners and we all laughed. Everything would be all right. It was in God's hands. The nurse continued.

"When the family has all arrived and you are ready, we will remove the respirator and give her a mild injection that will help her relax, then we wait. Sometimes they go relatively fast, and sometimes it takes several hours. Either way, we will have a nurse there to monitor her and make sure she is comfortable. Again, I want to reiterate, this will all be on your timing. Please feel free to ask any questions, to make any comments or to go as fast or as slow as you wish. It's your call. Any questions?"

"I don't have any, do you, Bub?" Deb asked looking at me. I shook my head.

As we were leaving, we all talked light-heartedly. Why wouldn't we? We were about to witness another of God's great miracles—the home going of our Mother. We were content with our decision.

The nurse walked us down to the Palliative Care Ward and introduced us to all the nurses there. We shared a chuckle with them. I had decided that God had blessed us so much on our journey up until now that I was not going to lose sight of that as we neared the end of this part of the adventure. I just knew that there was much more in store for us as time went on. This was not the end of the journey; just one more step along the path. Our cup had been filled to overflowing already. A tidal wave was still to come.

As she returned us to the Lounge, she said we should let them know when we wanted the machines to be removed.

"Will she still be with us after you do that?" one of the girls questioned.

"Oh yes. We won't start the rest of the process until we get her to P.C. and you tell us you are ready."

"OK, well then, I guess it's time. We'll go in for a visit, then you can begin that part of the process." I said it with complete confidence that it was the right thing to do. It had not been an easy decision, but Mom's living will and our conversations told me it was what needed to be done. She did not want us to prolong it when there was no real chance she'd survive it. The doctors gave us the best advice they could. We would have to trust them.

"If God is not ready for her, she will live through the machine removal and if He wants her, He will take her then. We can't lose." Deb's words rang so true now. I had really appreciated her saying that.

About 2:30, we went in to the ICU room that had been Mom's home for the previous week. The first time I had seen this place, it was so alive with the bustle of people, the machines making all the noises and the smell of antiseptic. Now, it had turned lifeless.

There was just the one nurse still tenderly caring for Mom and all her needs. The machines were beginning to be turned off. The tubes were being removed and the room didn't have the same antiseptic smell now. Along one side of the room there was a heater and a couple of chairs. Michael sat in one to rest. He was a real Godsend in all of this too. God knew what he was doing when He put those two together also.

Rachel and Arielle were with Noel in the Lounge. Finding things to keep a three year old busy for this long was not easy. But she is a good child and understood that Great-Grandma was very sick and needed for her to be very good.

Soon a P.C. nurse joined the ICU nurse and asked us if we'd like to go get something to eat or go to the Lounge. It would be about 20 minutes until they got Mom moved to her new room.

"Do you want to get something to eat?" Deb asked.

"I'm not all that hungry, but you go ahead if you want." I wasn't hungry, and still had a lot on my mind. I just wanted some time to think, meditate on the Lord and enjoy the thoughts of what was still to come.

"I think we'll take the girls and go down for a while then. Cheryl, how about you? You want to join us?"

"No thanks," my life partner responded. "I'll stay here with Randy. Tell Arielle to go ahead if she wants."

"OK, we'll be back in a few."

It was hard for Deb. She was trying to balance the needs of her husband, her daughter and especially, her grand daughter. When it was all said and done, she did it all with a great deal of grace and dignity. She never seemed overwhelmed, or flustered, or angry. I stopped for a moment and thanked God for that blessing too. It seemed I was in hypersensitivity mode. I was sensing all of God's blessings in everything. I thought back to that prayer that I had prayed just a week before.

"God, I don't understand why this has happened, but I thank you for it and ask for your guidance through it."

What a week! We had been blessed over and over again. We were about to be showered with more as Mom's family began to arrive. This would be the ride of a lifetime. "Grab your seat. Here we go!" I thought.

CHAPTER 18

"Do not let your hearts be troubled. Trust in God; trust also in Me. In my Father's house are many rooms; if it were not so, I would have told you. I am going there to prepare a place for you. And if I go and prepare a place for you, I will come back and take you to be with me that you also may be where I am."

– John 14:1-3 (NIV)

It was snowing South and East of Toledo that Wednesday afternoon. That was the direction all of her brothers and sisters were coming from. We found out when they arrived that some of the travel had been a little treacherous. I felt bad for them, but at least they had daylight in which to travel and all arrived safely.

The first to arrive were Uncle Ben and Aunt Miriam. Around 3:30, they came strolling in. We greeted them and Aunt Miriam approached Mom's bed as she had before. I had already decided that each of them would have as much time as they needed to say whatever they wanted to say. I stood back and watched her. My mind again shot back to the two of them as children and I smiled. This was so very difficult for Aunt Miriam. She had had Mom in her life the longest and recently they had gotten even closer than they had been before. They only lived about 10 miles apart and that allowed them a great deal of time together, especially after Dad died.

Uncle Ben and I stood away from the bed near the foot end and just talked softly. We had been close since I was in Junior High school. Uncle Ben was quite a woodworker with a great wood shop in his basement. He worked with me on my 4-H projects and helped me build a Cedar lined hope chest for my then fiancé. He was good at it and a good teacher too. Nothing was allowed to be "close enough". If it wasn't perfect, it wasn't right.

A couple of years after Mom's crash, Uncle Ben and Aunt Miriam would be in a wreck where a man came left of center and hit them head on. "I could only think of what happened to your Mother," was all he could say in a voice broken with emotion.

We chatted a bit and when Aunt Miriam looked up with misty eyes from her thoughts, we talked about what would happen and invited them to stay or leave at any point they wanted to. Aunt Miriam asked a couple of questions and I answered them along with Deb's help. She was always good at "interpreting" what I said so other people understood. Sometimes my mind gets in front of my tongue and the words come out in the wrong order. Deb always spoke "Randy" and could decipher the words into "normal English". Cheryl has that gift too. Good thing for me!

We had a nice conversation for a few minutes. I heard more feet in the hallway. Since Mom was the only one in the P.C. ward, I figured it had to be another of her siblings. It was her younger brother Uncle Wayne and his wife Aunt Janice. Again, there were greetings all around. I explained what was to happen as Uncle Wayne and Aunt Janice stood by Mom's bed.

"She looks different without all the tubes and machines," he said.

"Yea, they removed all those before they brought her down here. They only left the ventilator and one IV port. They will remove the ventilator when it's time and use the port to introduce the muscle relaxer to make her comfortable."

"When are you going to do that?"

"I wanted to wait until every one is here. Do you know if Uncle Chuck is going to be able to be here?" I asked.

"I'm not sure," said Aunt Janice, "but I think so."

"Oh good," was Deb's response, "I'm glad he will be here."

We stood back and gave them both their time with Mom. They had grown fairly close to her as well. Several years before, they had made a pact with Mom and Dad to go to lunch together on a regular monthly basis. That had worked well because even after Dad passed away, Mom continued her monthly outings with them. It was a good way for her to reattach with her "baby brother", as she occasionally called him. Usually it was with a mischievous smile on her face.

Just as they were finishing saying their goodbyes, another set of footsteps and another set of voices could be heard in the hallway. Appearing at the door were Aunt Linda, Aunt Carol and Uncle Bob. They had had quite a trip due to the weather and the roads, but in Aunt Carol's words, "We are here now. That's all that is important." Truer words were never spoken.

"We are just glad everyone can make it. I take it Uncle Chuck is coming too. Were you able to get in touch with him?" I asked.

"Yes, he will be here. He had to get Chuckie to come and stay with Mindy. He said as soon as he got the arrangements made, he'd be here."

"That's great."

As Aunt Carol approached the bed, you could see in her body language the sorrow come over her. Her shoulders slumped as she and Aunt Linda stood with their arms around each other looking at their eldest sister. As I watched them, I was struck by the affection between them. It was exactly the scenario I had envisioned when I suggested we wait for all of her siblings to be by her side when we all said goodbye. We would all be together because of her. She would like that. Her family was so important to her and having them all together in one place at one time will be so special.

"Thank you for including us," Aunt Carol said as she turned back around toward Deb and I. "It means a lot. You have done a good job of keeping us informed throughout this whole ordeal and we appreciate that."

"We've done the best we could in a difficult situation. We are glad you all can be here with her."

The P.C. nurse came in. "Is everyone here, yet?"

"No, we have one more brother to see yet." I then proceeded to introduce every one to Nurse J. "Wow, quite a family! It's nice to meet all of you. There is a small waiting room across the hall which you can all use as you wish. There is pop, water and juice in the refrigerator and coffee in the coffee pot. Help yourselves to anything you want. If you need anything else, please ask. We are here for you." With that, she checked the ventilator and left quietly. Some of our "crew" retired to the waiting room, while a couple stayed there with us. I wanted to wait for Uncle Chuck. I didn't have to wait long.

Soon he shuffled in with his wife in tow. When he first arrived at the door, I didn't recognize him. I saw, instead, a smaller version of my maternal Grandfather. Grandpa was a large man of German descent. His shoes always seemed to me to be as large as a luxury liner and his coats looked big enough that all of his grandchildren could fit in it all at the same time. Uncle Chuck has many of the same mannerisms, nearly the same facial features and the same build as Grandpa, just a little smaller.

"Hi Uncle Chuck," I said, "I'm glad you are here. Hello, Aunt Mindy, I'm glad you were able to come."

I was a bit surprised to see her. She had not been well for a period of time before Mom's wreck and I wasn't even sure she would be able to be her with us. I was certainly happy that she was.

After explaining what was to happen from here on, I gave them their time with Mom too. Uncle Chuck was visibly shaken. It was not a response I would have expected from him. He had always seemed like the stoic one in the family. He was the oldest of the boys and much of the farm work had fallen on his shoulders in his early years. He handled the fieldwork and Grandpa did most of the work with the animals, although, they shared both parts of the farm operations. Of all of Mom's siblings, he was the one I knew the least well. Not that I didn't know him, I just wasn't as close to him as the rest. I don't know why, that's just the way it was.

His children both attended high school where I taught and coached for a while in the early part of my career. His son, Chuck, Jr., whom the family all called Chuckie, played football on one of the teams I coached. Chuckie's younger sister, Heidi, was a cheerleader for a while in Junior High and early High School. I had taught both of them in my science classes. I knew them better, probably, in my professional duties as a teacher, coach and athletic director than I did as members of the same family.

When they had finished, I went into the waiting area and told them all we were going to get started soon, so if they had anything else they wanted to say, they should do so now. I stayed there as they each went in one-by-one, often with their spouses, and said their final goodbyes. It was their time with her, I had had mine, Deb's family had had theirs, and our "girls" had had theirs too, so now it was Mom's siblings' turn. I knew they would be fine, but they each needed and wanted "alone" time. It was only right. Throughout all of this, that was the biggest challenge. Making the right decision at the right time for the right reasons for all the right people was difficult. By God's grace and with His blessing, we had done a pretty fair job of it. Everyone that needed to be here was here. They would be able to say anything to Mom they needed to and that was good. God was blessing us even more now. Our whole family was in one place and would be part of a major life-changing event. God is good.

After each of them had finished, I went to the nurses' desk and told Nurse J we were ready. It was time. We all circled around Mom's bed and held hands. I felt to the greatest degree I ever had, the presence of the Holy Spirit there in that room. The love for Mom and the love of our Lord filled that space. Michael prayed and I prayed and when we all said, "Amen," I felt a huge weight release from shoulders. It was time to let Mom go.

As we watched, Nurse J slowly and gently removed the ventilator from Mom. She offered that any who wished could stay, but Arielle had couldn't watch and she left. She told us later, it was just too hard. A couple of her Aunts and Uncles agreed and left for a few minutes.

As Aunt Linda and I stood by Mom's bedside, arms around each other, the ventilator removed, my Aunt looked at me and said, "Look, she's smiling."

It was true. Mom had just the slightest upturn at the corner of her mouth.

"She's ready to go now," Aunt Linda said.

"Yes she is." It was all I could think to say, and all we needed to say.

Mom's breathing was shallow and irregular, but continued. Nurse J came in and gave the muscle relaxant through the only port left in Mom's right hand. Within a minute, her breathing became steadier, albeit, more labored. It was about 5:30.

By 7:00 she was breathing more slowly but seemed very peaceful. Her brothers and sisters began leaving at that point. They wanted to get at least part of the way home while it was still light. Praise God that for their safe trip home, it was no longer snowing and the snow plows had done their work.

As they left, each one hugged us and thanked us for including them in these last few minutes of Mom's life. We appreciated the positive comments but it was really the right thing to do and I couldn't have imagined it being done any other way. It was beautiful, it was dignified and it was done with family—just like Mom.

It was Deb who finally broke the silence that had settled over our two families when she said, "Mom would be happy her brothers and sisters were here."

"She sure is," I replied. "They are glad they were here, too." Everyone nodded. There was not much to say. Now we would just wait.

"Mom, it's OK, you can go now." I was thinking it, but I'm pretty sure I said it aloud, because Deb said it too. We were ready, and so was she.

I realized at that moment that I felt more peaceful and Mom looked more peaceful than either of us had been for the last week. She was going to see her Lord and I was comfortable with placing her in God's holy hands. She was going to be better off in that world, than in this one. I was proud of her and of the person into whom she had made me. A tear slipped down my cheek, but it was not a tear of sorrow. It was an emotional tear. I was not even sure what emotion it was. I still don't know exactly. I just felt so overwhelmed, so overcome with feelings, that I guess that was the only way my body knew how to release it.

In the last week, I had gone through the entire gamut of emotions. Shock, anger, love, hate, joy, pain, and sorrow had all enveloped me at different times through the week. Now, there was, to a certain degree, relief. I had resigned myself to the idea that Mom was leaving, and by God's grace and his many blessings I was all right with that.

He had a plan and I had to accept that. I had to accept that nothing is done in our time, by our guidelines or because of something we want. His plan is better than anything we could develop. God had handled every little detail all along the way. What more could I ask for? His plan, His timing, and His way—what else was there? Mom was needed in Heaven, and we were needed to tell her story here. It really was that simple. Soon it would be complete but not until God said it was time.

There was no sense of sadness in the room. Michael had taken it upon himself, consciously or unconsciously, to keep this a celebration of Mom. I had promised her in one of our conversations that there would not be a lot of crying and wailing at her funeral, whenever that was. She wanted it to be a celebration of her life and her accomplishments for the Kingdom. I would make sure of that at her funeral. Now, we were laughing, chuckling, and telling stories about Mom and the things we had done together that were probably not always things she would be proud of. At various times, one would go and spend some time with Noel so the others could be part of what was happening.

It was nearing midnight and Mom was nearly gone. The breathing was slowing and extremely shallow. Nurse J came in and told us it would not be long. We all circled Mom's bed again and as Nurse J began to step back, I reached for her hand and asked her to join us if she'd like to. She nodded.

Michael prayed, *"Lord, we offer up Mom's spirit to You now. She is coming to be with You and Dad. We are so grateful for the time we've had with her here, and now we look forward to the time when we will all be with both of you in Glory. Lord, give us peace and memories of the joy she brought us while on this earth and wrap Your loving arms around her when You greet her there. We love her and we love You. In your name we pray, Amen."*

Nurse J hung onto my hand for a moment more, and I realized she was sniffling. I asked her quietly if she was all right.

"Yes, you guys are incredible. What a loving and blessed family! She had to have been a great lady to have raised such an inspiring family."

We had heard that comment before.

"I guess this is the best way to honor Mom," I thought. "I know she would be proud."

Nurse J was one of the sweetest, kindest, most caring people we had met since we had arrived about a week before. Her tenderness toward Mom and our family was genuine. There was nothing phony about her.

"I don't normally get this emotional or this involved with the families we serve, but I just can't help it with you guys."

"Yea, we have that effect on a lot of people," Mike quipped and we all laughed.

We had a great time there praising God, remembering Mom and talking with the nurses. We told them a few of the stories of our shenanigans and Mom's reaction to most of them were the same. We would get "the look", then she'd try to keep a straight face and stare us down, then that large beautiful smile would come across her and we'd all start laughing. If someone had said anything a little bit embarrassing, we might also get a little flush of pink on her face as well. We all laughed about that.

Just before midnight, as we all stood at her bedside, Mom's breathing slowed to less than three times per minute. At a minute or so after midnight, she took her last breath. God's timing had come. She was with Him now.

"We have to wait ten more minutes," said Nurse J.

Ten minutes later as she stood with us there at our Mother's bedside, she pronounced my Mother had passed away at 12:10 AM, Thursday, March 31, 2011. Her pain was over and God was welcoming her home.

"Praise God from whom all blessings flow," Deb began to sing and we all joined in. "Praise Him all creatures here below. Praise Him above ye heavenly host. Praise Father, Son and Holy Ghost."

It had been an important song for our entire family throughout our childhood and adult lives. We sang it every Sunday in that little country church just down the road and often sang it at family reunions in place of a meal prayer. It seemed appropriate now and I was glad the Holy Spirit laid it on Deb's heart. It was perfect at that moment. Another blessing came raining down on us from above. It was a great moment in time. Mom would be happy. She was in her house of many rooms where she would dwell with the Lord forever. She would praise Him for all eternity.

"In my Father's house are many rooms; ...I am going to prepare a place for you." The words from John 14:2 raced through my mind. Jesus had prepared the place for her, and now she was going there for all eternity.

CHAPTER 19

*"And pray in the Spirit on all occasions with
all kinds of prayers and requests. With this in
mind, be alert and always keep on praying for
all the saints."*

– Ephesians 6:18 (NIV)

We remained in her room for a few more minutes and then we
each kissed Mom goodbye and left. We chatted a few minutes
in the lounge and then Cheryl, Arielle and I walked Deb, Mike,
Rachel and Noel down to the elevator and out toward the lobby.
We discussed the arrangements.

Among the many responsibilities I had during these last few hours
was to let the hospital know which funeral service we wanted to
use. They would call and make the arrangements to have the body
released to them. We chose the local funeral home where Dad had
been when he passed away a couple of years earlier. They are great
people and extremely professional. It has been a family owned
business for what is now four generations. Most of the funerals
in my family have been held there. The funeral director is an old
friend of mine, the same as his father was a friend of Dad's. Gus
had been an outstanding high school basketball player and was
well known in the community.

We walked Deb's family to their car on our way to our room. It was late and they would stay one more night in the hotel and we would spend our last night in our "Home Away From Home". We would meet up in the morning, and go to the funeral home together. Mike and Deb could camp out at our place during the day, but they planned to spend the rest of the weekend at Michael's parents' home in Mansfield. They would only be a forty-minute drive away, but it would work well because we were going to have a house full.

Arielle, Cheryl and I walked slowly back to our room. I was so glad to have them here with me. Since Arielle had moved to college, then to West Virginia, I had missed her more than I had ever let on. We sat on the edge of the bed together and had a huge "group hug" that warmed us all. I recognized again, how important family is. I needed them there with me and they were. Praise God for this blessing too.

We got ready for bed and set an alarm so we could get a good start in the morning.

"Thank you Lord for what you've done today. I still don't completely understand it, but I know that You will bless us for being faithful to You. Be with Shawn's family tonight and throughout the coming weeks. This will be tough on him and his family. Give him healing. In Your name, Amen."

I needed to pray for us, but even more, right now I needed to pray for him. I was sure, based on what Mark had told me about him, that Shawn would be torn up inside about this. I wanted him to know that no one blamed him for the wreck. He is a good man of high moral character and I had prayed for him because he needed it. Nothing more than that was required. We should pray for those in need, no matter what the situation and pray constantly. He was hurting, he needed prayer and I was just being faithful to my God and Father who had commanded us to do so. The verse from Ephesians 6:18 came to mind and I mumbled it to remind me.

As Deb and I talked later, we both made a concerted effort to love on him and his family as Jesus would have loved on us if we were in the same situation. It was not easy, but nothing worth doing is easy. I reminded myself daily that Mom would have set the same example for us if any of these events had been different. She would have scolded us, as only a Mother can, if we had been any other way. It was difficult for us, but we relied on each other to provide support throughout the coming months and we were able to show His love, through our love. That was a blessing also. Praise Him.

It was late when we retired to our room, but I was able to rise refreshed and ready to go home. We had been told last night that the funeral home would be picking Mom up overnight. I felt good that she was getting back to the town where she had spent most of her adult life. That seemed to me to be some sense closure, too. She would be there by the time we met with Gus. I called on my way home and we set up our appointment for 10 AM. Deb thought that would work for them too.

Arielle and Cheryl rode home together and I led the way. I needed some time alone. I began to think about the timing of the calling hours, the funeral and whether PB would be available to do the funeral. I also realized that I still had some phone calls to make to friends. I called Mark to let him know Mom was gone, and that I would let him know about arrangements after we were done at Gus's.

The "norm" for funerals is usually 3 days after the passing, but that would have been Sunday. When Deb and I talked, we didn't want to do that. So, it was decided we would have calling hours on Friday and the funeral on Saturday. I asked Gus if this was going to be a problem for him.

"No, we can make that happen," he responded.

During our chat with Gus, we ran through his checklist to make sure we got everything covered. One of the hardest parts was writing the obituary. We wanted to include as much of the pertinent information in it without "overdoing" it. I think we did a pretty good job. The collaboration between Michael, Cheryl, Deb and I provided a good summary without being overblown. I was very proud of my sister and the way she was handling all of this. She was a rock—at least on the outside and at least right now.

We finished the paperwork and proceeded to the room where the caskets were on display. It was familiar to me, because just a short time before I had been there with Mom to choose Dad's casket. She had seen a simple pink one that she had really liked for herself and it was the same model as Dad's blue one.

"That is only fitting," I thought. I mentioned it to Deb.

"I like that one two. I like the outside color and the light pastel pink will go well with the outfit I want to give them to bury her in." With that it was decided.

"OK," Gus said as he entered the room, "have you made a decision?"

We discussed the casket and all the other things that went with it.

"We will be ready then for calling hours tomorrow night."

As we left the funeral home, I noticed some sadness in Deb's eyes. I'm sure she would say the same about me if someone had asked. It all seemed so final now. It really was almost over.

Deb and Mike along with Rachel and Noel, made plans to go to Mansfield to his parents' house for the weekend. They would be leaving from the farm after we got Mom's dress for Gus. As they pulled out of the drive of the funeral home, I prayed again.

"Thank you Lord for putting Michael in Deb's life. He is exactly what she needs right now. His spirit is strong and he knows what to say, how to say it and when to say it. Bless them as they travel back and forth this weekend. Thank you for what you are doing with all the details. Keep Arielle safe in her travels too. In Jesus Name, Amen."

The little prayer for Arielle was because she had left earlier in the morning to return to West Virginia. She needed more clothes and she needed Josh. At that point, she needed his strength and friendship. The hardest thing for a father is "giving up" his little girl. Mothers and Daughters have a very special bond, but this Father-Daughter bond is really something special. When I finally realized that she and Josh were serious, it hurt a little. Honestly, a little bit of me hurt pretty badly. Then I came to the realization that it was all part of the circle of life, and I'm proud of the young man she's chosen to be her life partner. God had his hand in that and Josh truly is a blessing to our family and especially to her. He is all I could ask for in a future son-in-law and I'm full of joy that they are together.

Cheryl and I went to the farm with Deb and Mike to get the dress the girls had chosen for Mom. It was one of my favorites too. It was a light teal colored dress that Mom had purchased for my daughter's graduation from college. It was special for Arielle too. The girls had chosen the perfect dress for Mom to wear to greet her Lord and Savior. Her wings would look excellent with it.

So many blessings had continued to rain down on us the last few days, but we never imagined what it would be like the next few days. Blessings were coming fast and furious and we could only hold on for the ride. God had tremendous plans for us and we were about to get drenched again with His holiness and magnificence.

When we got home around 1:00 there were at least twenty messages on our answering machine. I carefully wrote down all the messages and return numbers. If all these people were kind enough to call, the least I could do was to return those calls. I started by calling Mark and Aunt Janice. They had done such a great job of contacting folks during the past week, I continued using them to spread the word of the arrangements. They did it and did it well.

Each of the calls I made was important, both to the caller and to me. I received the usual condolences and well wishes and the comment, "If there is anything we can do, please call." I knew I wouldn't, but I thanked them anyway. I found out later that a couple of the calls I returned kicked off a world-wide call chain, because Mom and Dad had been involved with a Silver King Tractor Club that had members all over the planet. In fact, Dad and one of his cousins had actually teamed up with a couple of people from Plymouth to start the club. Plymouth was the town in which the factory that made the Silver King tractors was located. The small village is only about eight miles from the family farm. Dad was quite a collector of the old relics and was extremely knowledgeable about them. Word of Mom's passing had spread quickly through the group to Europe and New Zealand. That was cool!

While I made the calls, Cheryl fixed us a light lunch. When we were finished, I sat down and just relaxed on the couch. It was good to be home again. It was good to be away from the hospital, the nurses, the doctors, the machines and the hustle and bustle of the place. Don't get me wrong, it was as good an experience as it could have been given the circumstances, but I was tired and needed to rest away from it all. Cheryl sat next to me on the couch and we chatted for a while.

"Why don't you close your eyes and rest for a while? You look really tired." She was right. I was tired. I was weary from everything we had been through since last Thursday. Now, a week later, I was finally resting, in my loving wife's arms warm and safe from the world. I dozed off to sleep. As I drifted off, I had one more prayer.

"Lord, thank You for the time we had with our Mother. I know she's there with You right now. Please hold her and let her know we will be all right down here. Be with the rest of my family too and especially guide and protect Arielle as she travels this weekend. Thank You for being in control of every detail in all of this and for the bounteous blessings You've laid on me. In Jesus Name, Amen."

CHAPTER 20

"Jesus replied, 'If anyone loves me, he will obey my teaching. My Father will love him, and we will come to him and make our home in him."

— John 14:23 (NIV)

I was awakened from my deep sleep by the ringing of our landline phone. It was Arielle.

"Hi, I made it," came the familiar voice on the other end.

"How was your trip?" her mother asked.

"Pretty good, not too much traffic. Josh and I will be coming home tomorrow night after he gets off work. We should be leaving here by about 3 or so. He talked to his boss and they are letting him come in early so he can leave early and they are giving him Monday off, too, but he needs to be back for class. I talked to my boss and he told me they are giving me 2 extra days of bereavement leave so I won't miss any time without pay."

Another God sighting was in the works. His blessings were raining down on my daughter and her boyfriend too.

"Wow, that's terrific, sounds like everyone is really cooperating with you guys down there."

"Yep, God is handling everything," said Arielle. I was very proud of her for recognizing it.

"Josh's grandparents wanted to know where to send flowers."

"Tell them we are asking for donations to Habitat for Humanity or any charity they want to choose. We aren't doing a lot of flowers," I responded.

"Rachel and I can do some though, right?" Arielle's voice almost broke when she asked the question. I could hear the disappointment in her response.

"Oh sure, honey," I said. "Aunt Deb and I just think it is more to the point to have donations made to a charity that your Grandma was involved in rather than on flowers that don't do as much good for as many people. You know how important her work with Murray and Habitat was to her."

"Yea Murray was really into that and Grandma got into it too."

Murray was a life-long friend of the family. He had lost his wife several years prior to Dad's passing. Betty and Murray had attended church with our family and they, too, had been foster parents. They had served over 70 children during their lifetimes. Some were short-term and many were long-term. They had a couple of kids while we were all in high school and we became very close to them. Charlie and Alma were brother and sister, were both about my age and were quickly adopted into our Youth Group at church. They became viable and active members of the group. Murray had been very lonely after his wife died and he and Mom "dated" for a while before he passed away. Mom was very sad that she had lost another "dear friend" as she called him. They were good for each other.

As Arielle said her goodbyes to us, she promised to call before she went to bed for the night. She has always done that. I don't remember a time she didn't call. Even through college and the move to West Virginia, she always called us before she retired for the night. It's always great to hear her voice. We have a little saying that we say to each other before she goes to sleep. It is, "Goodnight, sweet dreams-big fields and pretty butterflies."

It came from a time when she was just less than two years old. She had a bad dream and couldn't go back to sleep. We sat with her and I said to her that she should think of something nice right before she goes to sleep.

So, on the spot, I just said, "Think of a great big field with lots of flowers and pretty butterflies flying around you. That will help you sleep better."

The next night, she said to me as she was going to bed, "Daddy, do big fields and pretty butterflies, again." So, it just stuck. Every night we close our day with "Big fields and pretty butterflies. Love you honey." It seems silly, but it's part of who this huge-hearted daughter of mine is, and why we have such an incredible relationship.

The rest of the evening we just sat with the TV on. I'm not sure that I even watched it. I was there, with my wife, at home and that was all that I needed right then. About 10 o'clock, she asked me if I was ready for bed. I told her I was and added, "We have a long day tomorrow and Saturday." Little did I know then that

God wasn't finished blessing us yet. There was more to come. But, at least I was in my home, with my wife and my Lord. Life is good.

CHAPTER 21

"For surely, O Lord, you bless the righteous;
you surround them with your favor as with a
shield."

– Psalm 5:12 (NIV)

We had set calling hours for 4:00 on Friday. We decided to go straight through until 9:00 rather than taking a break. I wanted to make sure that all the people who wanted to visit would have the chance. It would be a long haul for the family, but we had several people tell us how much they appreciated it.

Gus had told us the funeral parlor would be open all the time, but the calling hours simply meant the times when the family would be there to greet the visitors. I hadn't realized that before, but it was good to know.

We had been provided with a room upstairs that had a kitchen, a table with chairs and a couple of large chairs that we could use as a retreat if we needed one. It was comfortable and away from the bustle. We put a large cold meat tray that had been provided for us up there. That was another blessing. It gave our family a way to grab something light to eat without having to leave the funeral home.

Cheryl and I got there around 2:30, more because I didn't want to sit around the house than anything. Gus greeted us and with him was Jessica. She is a student studying the business and was interning with Gus. I had had Jessica in school when she was in Junior High. She is a lovely girl with a great personality and a cordial, warm way about her that makes her perfect for the field she's chosen.

A few people trickled in early, and we greeted them as they arrived. Over the next five and a half hours we would receive so many blessings, greetings and well wishes that my heart was about to explode.

Around 4:30 or so, a large contingent of my co-workers appeared. My boss, the secretaries and several of the teachers and coaches had made the trek. It was good of them to come. Their expressions of kindness were great, but just having them be there meant so much. As they passed through the reception line, each made a kind comment and my boss told me to take as much time as I needed to get things settled. I thanked him and told him I really appreciated it. It was good to see them.

Many of the people who came through were friends of Mom's from her younger days, while some were family relatives I had not seen in years. But all wished us the best and passed on through the line. We had chosen to have the casket closed because of the facial injuries Mom had suffered. It seemed appropriate and I don't regret it at all. We placed a large bust picture of Mom in a nice gold frame on the casket beside the peach colored roses from Rachel and Arielle. There was also a single yellow rose that Noel had placed on the casket as well. It was important to her and we all agreed.

Not much of this made much sense to Noel; she just knew that Great-Grandma was in heaven. For quite some time afterward, and even until now, she talks about the ways she and Great-Grandma did this or that. They were so close, and I was glad that Noel had gotten to spend that time with her.

As the night went on, all of Mom's siblings came through the line then took a seat at one of the many couches and chairs around the spacious room. It was good to have them all together again in one place. They were able to socialize with each other, as were many of our cousins who, because of busy life styles, maybe don't see as much of one another as they would like. The place was abuzz with activity. There was exactly what I had hoped for—a celebration of Mom's life. I tried to stay as upbeat as possible, as I was laughing at stories people told, smiling at all I greeted and generally trying to talk about the good things that had happened since the crash. I did not want this to become a quiet somber time. I wanted to celebrate her life, not mourn her death.

Suddenly, there in the doorway, stood several teachers from Monroeville, the school at which I had taught just three years prior. There were at least six of them that had come to visit our family at this time of our need. I had always been very fortunate to be surrounded by great people at all the schools at which I worked. This was no exception.

When Dad had passed away, I was still teaching at Monroeville. Dad had been adopted by the football team as a kind of "Grandpa" to all of them. He was in the latter stages of his life as a result of kidney disease and a couple of different bouts of cancers and they had accepted him into the fold. We were fairly successful at that time and made the playoffs a couple of times. One of Dad's proudest moments was having his picture taken with the team after one of our playoff wins.

During his calling hours, and unbeknown to me, the entire team had boarded a bus and had come to visit, dressed in ties and football jerseys. It was an incredible tribute for them to show this kind of love and caring for Dad. That was an example of the kind of kids and the kind of program they had at Monroeville. Now, the Head Football coach, several of the assistant coaches and many of the teachers from Monroeville were here for Mom, too. Wow. What a blessing!

Around 8:00, Arielle and Josh came in. The trip had been good with fairly light traffic. I paused for a moment to thank God for a safe trip for them. It was good to have her there, and she was glad to have Josh with her. They made a good couple standing in the line greeting people she knew. And ever the gracious person, always talking to the ones she didn't know. Most introduced themselves, and the ones that didn't, either Deb or I would introduce.

The line continued to grow and more and more people came through the doors. It was great to see all of them, to meet those I didn't know and reacquaint with those we had not seen in a very long time. It went on until nearly 10 PM. I was thrilled, but very tired at the end of the night. Tomorrow was the funeral. I could only hope it would be a celebration of her life too. That's the way Mom would want it.

I kissed Deb goodnight and Cheryl and I went to our truck, while Josh and Arielle went to her car. I noticed he opened the door for her and let her in, then went around to the driver's side and climbed in. He was treating her well and I was glad for that. She had done well choosing a man with which she could share her life.

When we got home, we went straight to bed. Cheryl had taken some time earlier in the day to make up the guest room for Josh. Arielle would do fine in her old room. It was good to have her home again. It didn't take long for all of us to be asleep. We would have another big day tomorrow.

I prayed just before my slumber overtook me.

"Lord, thank You for all those people You brought along our path tonight. Bless each one for blessing us. You are a marvelous God and You are so good to us. Thank You for tonight and bless us as we show Your love throughout the trials and tribulations still to come. In His Name, Amen."

CHAPTER 22

"The Spirit of the Sovereign Lord is on me, because the Lord has anointed me to preach good news to the poor. He has sent me to bind up the brokenhearted...to comfort all who mourn, and provide for those who grieve...to bestow on them a crown of beauty instead of ashes, the oil of gladness instead of mourning, and a garment of praise instead of a spirit of despair. They will be called oaks of righteousness, a planting of the Lord for the display of his splendor."

– Isaiah 61:1-3 (NIV)

By 9:30 AM the funeral home was already starting to fill with friends and family. "More than I would have guessed," I thought.

"There are a lot of people here," I said to Cheryl. "I didn't think there would be this many."

"Your mother was an incredible person and she touched a lot of people. Did you really think no one would show up?" she said in a mocking voice with a smile on her face. I smiled back at her and realized I should have known it would be "busting at the seams" with people. She was a great person and these folks were here to pay tribute to her life. I was bound and determined we would do that without the sorrow.

We had asked Pastor Bob and Pastor Pete to do the honors of officiating the service. Pastor Pete was the lay minister for Mom's church. We had discussed with Michael if he was interested in being part of it and he quietly declined. It was OK, but I thought we should make the offer.

It was a celebration. We sang praise songs and people had the opportunity to respond with favorite stories or anecdotes about Mom. Rachel and Arielle did an "ABC's of Grandma". They described her using letters of the alphabet and a short explanation of each one. Some parts of it were very funny, some were more somber, but they were thoughts from the hearts of her two favorite girls. It was very touching and in its own way, very celebratory. It was *their* memories of *their* Grandmother stated in *their own* words. They had done the same for Dad at his funeral, and this one was just as good. Blessings filled the room as some individuals sang along, while some sat in quiet reflection and others were smiling as they remembered one or more of the ways Mom had touched their lives. It was great. I was sure Mom was pleased. It was a God-filled time to honor a God-filled person. Praise His holy name for the blessings of the day.

I have included, at the end of the book, the girls' tribute and that of Deb, to show the depth of their love for her. This book would not be complete without those blessings too.

At the conclusion of the service, the pallbearers loaded the casket into the hearse and as we pulled out of town toward the cemetery, I realized that Gus was not going directly there. He was detouring past the farm. It wasn't really that much of a detour, but it was a nice touch. The entire funeral procession was following us for a final pass by the farm where Mom had spent most of her adult life. It was a fitting tribute and I was glad Gus had thought of it. We had done the same for Dad a couple years prior; Gus remembered and did the same for Mom. "Nice touch, Gus," I thought as we drove by the old homestead. "Very appropriate."

We had the service at the cemetery then returned to Mom's church just up the road about two miles for a meal served by the members of her church family. It was a nice social gathering and a good release. Most of her siblings were there and I enjoyed hearing their stories, laughter and joy as they shared with each other and other family and friends that had joined us. Blessings flowed over me as I sat back and heard them celebrating her life—just as I had hoped. It had been a good day. Mom was in her final resting place, next to Dad, and was with him and her Godly Father in heaven. What else was left to do other than commemorate her life in our hearts and minds? They loved her, we loved her and God loved her. It was a fitting end to a perfect day. God had taken care of every detail. Praise Him for that.

When we finished at the church, Deb and Mike followed us back to our house and we just sat and talked. We didn't have a particular agenda, but we just talked about the future, the farm, the trust and life in general. It was great to talk to her with no particular reason or direction for the conversation. We were both tired but jubilant at the same time because of what we had just witnessed. They left a couple of hours later to go back to Columbus. I would miss them. Feeling their support throughout the last week and a half had been so great. God knew what he was doing when he gave me this family. I had to let him be in charge of the rest too.

I slept better that night than any since this journey began. It was all over and now I could go back to some normalcy in my life. Well, not exactly. God wasn't done with blessing me yet. He still had more to prove. Much more. I think He really expected me to follow through with the directive I had received in that waiting room—I had to write a book. He expected me to display His splendor. I would have to obey.

CHAPTER 23

*"Direct my footsteps according to your word; let
no sin rule over me."*

– Psalm 119:133 (NIV)

Our church is very welcoming and friendly. The people there really
care for each other, whether they are the original members, or have
never been in the church before. We felt so warm and comforted
by the congregation in the loss of Mom. Arielle and Josh were with
us and we sat together near the front. The message rained down on
me and brought me a great deal of comfort. It was exactly what I
needed, exactly when I needed it, and in exactly the right amount.
God and I were handling this, just like He promised. There were
believers there to help surround me and immerse me in His love.
His strength and compassion shone through in each face that
greeted us. They loved on Arielle and Josh too, and that certainly
meant a lot to them.

Following church we went to have some lunch before Josh and
Arielle headed back home. I was sad to see them go, but they
needed to return to their normal too. We kissed her goodbye and
with hugs and wishes for safe travel, we sent them on their way.
God had them in His control and they would be just fine.

Sunday is normally a lazy day for me. I can usually find time for a "short" two to three hour nap in the afternoon. This Sunday was no different. I rested well even if it was longer than I should have slept. My father-in-law was quite a NASCAR fan and, as we grew closer I had become one too—sort of. When I watched a race, I would usually see the first few laps, fall sound asleep and watch the last three laps. Dick had always been a Dale Earnhardt fan, and after Earnhardt's death in a racing accident, Dick became a Dale, Jr. fan. I was too, but watching every lap of any race was difficult, so I usually slept through most of them. After church that Sunday, we came home and I assumed my normal Sunday afternoon position on the couch. I didn't see either the start or the end of the race, only the backs of my eyelids.

The next several months were hectic with meeting with lawyers and getting death certificates, canceling social security benefits and credit cards while trying to guard against identity theft, and, oh yea, working. Mom and Dad had seen a lawyer to set up a trust for the farm. They felt it was the only way to protect the assets if either one ever needed an extended stay facility. It should have been pretty straightforward process to settle the estate, but because she died as a result of the injuries from the wreck, it complicated matters. But, not to worry, eventually, in His timing, God would take care of it.

It wasn't always easy to turn all of it over to Him, but I did, and it all worked out in the end. He empowered me to be bold at the right times and to be subjective to others when needed. Knowing how to do that was not always my strong suit. He provided me with good advisors and blessing after blessing with the service representatives for each stage along the way. I had every conceivable blessing come my way. Although at times I got frustrated with all the paperwork, God was in charge. As long as I focused on Him, someone a lot more in charge than I would work out all the details. He did, and I praised Him for it every day.

My first day back to work was hectic with many visitors from among our teaching and coaching staffs, meetings with Brad and Linda and preparing for the day's athletic events. I answered messages and when Lisa dropped by, she brought me up to speed on everything I had missed. She, as I have mentioned before, was a great blessing to me. I was so thankful that God had put her in that position a couple of years before.

As time went along, each day got a little bit easier. I began the process of finalizing all the financial requirements to close out the estate. Little did I know it would be nearly three years until it was all finished. I met with lawyers and bankers. Sent letters and correspondences all over the U.S. to get what I needed. Mom had been very organized, but there was still a great deal of unfinished business left hanging.

In the process of working through the financial requirements, we had to inventory Mom's business. Mom had owned a small business selling knitting machines, embroidery machines and custom-made items she had made with both. Dad had been her "technician" until he got sick enough he couldn't do it anymore. It was a great "Mom and Pop" operation for them to do together. They had an excellent time going to fairs, shows and conferences and it was wonderful for them to be able to spend time collectively.

God sent us another blessing by providing us with the names of some ladies that knew the machines and their values, as well as the value of all the yarn, thread and supplies Mom had in stock. They were able to give us fair market value of the items so we could include it in the probate process. Additionally, God provided us with a very good friend who was a farmland appraiser. Don (not the same one that made the first call to me) and his wife Sandy are excellent cattlemen, and have been great friends of ours for several years. He was more than willing to appraise the farm for us. He knew it well, because his kids and Arielle had been in 4-H together and he had helped her greatly with her cattle. It was good to have someone to trust at times like these. Don also handled Mom's auction when the time came for that. Their support came along when we needed it and they were a great blessing too.

God was in control of everything. He was controlling all of our footsteps and guiding us along the path He wanted us to travel. Blessings and more blessings fell on us daily as we walked in Him and by His plan.

CHAPTER 24

"Do not judge, and you will not be judged. Do not condemn, and you will not be condemned. Forgive, and you will be forgiven. Give, and it will be given to you. A good measure, pressed down, shaken together and running over, will be poured into your lap. For with the measure you use, it will be measured to you."

– Luke 6:37-38 (NIV)

This was a trying time for Shawn and his family. He had been charged through the legal system and was facing fines and jail time. Deb and I had already decided that the best way to show the love of God that our mother had instilled in us was to plead to the court for leniency. Shawn was, by all accounts, a good man, a great husband, a fantastic father and a strong man of God. He had made a very bad mistake. I found out later that he has paid for that mistake every day in his own mind. He needed us to show him the Love of God. If Christ can ask for forgiveness for the men who were crucifying Him, we should have been able to forgive Shawn for his mistake. We consciously chose to do that.

The court system has a counselor known as a "victim's advocate". That individual is responsible for walking the victim or the victim's family through the legal process and to keep them apprised as to what is happening with the defendant. Ours was incredible. She was a blessing that God placed in that place at that time for us. She led us selflessly and quietly through all the proceedings and was in constant contact with us regarding the case. She also served as a liaison between the prosecuting attorney, the defense attorney and us.

As part of the sentencing phase of the proceedings, we were permitted to address the court. We were allowed to make requests of the judge regarding our desires concerning Shawn's fate. The judge had the discretionary power to invoke the penalty based on any, all or none of our recommendations. We prayed for a judge that would listen and heed our desires. We were blessed that that was exactly what we got.

It was a cold, damp early December morning as I drove to the courthouse. Deb was unable to make it to court that day, so she sent me her victim's statement to read to the court. I was happy to do that. The emotions began to well up in me as I entered the courtroom. It was smaller than I expected. I guess I had seen so many movies and TV shows that I misjudged the size of a typical courtroom. I sat in the front row, near the middle, just behind a banister that went the width of the room. On a raised podium in front of me was the judges' bench with long wooden tables on either side. I noticed a microphone for the judge's use. Apparently, this was going to be taped.

When Shawn entered the courtroom to my left, his lawyer accompanied him. Seated beside me were the victim's advocate and several seats to her right and back a row was a lovely young woman. I had not met the family, but I was pretty sure it was Shawn's wife.

Sitting at the table opposite Shawn and his lawyer was the prosecutor. Both lawyers were dressed in nice suits and ties and fully looked the part. The door in the front opened and the judge walked in. We all stood up. A tall man with salt and pepper hair, dressed in a black robe entered and moved up the four steps to his perch. "You may be seated," he said as he reached to his right and pushed a button to record what was about to happen.

Shawn looked worn and tired. The previous few months had taken a toll on him physically. He stood before the judge but his shoulders told a story of a beaten man. My heart went out to him as he told his side of the story. He showed great remorse and sorrow during his statement. His lawyer asked for a plea change from "Guilty" to "No Contest". The judge was a little irritated at that because a plea deal had apparently all ready been struck. The judge queried the prosecutor as to his wishes and, finally, after some legal wrangling, the plea was accepted.

The judge asked if there was anyone in the courtroom who had anything to say before he pronounced the verdict. Barbara, my victim's advocate stood and introduced me and asked that I be allowed to address the court. The judge nodded. I rose and read my sister's victim's statement first. I have also included both victims' statements in the back of the book. Basically, we both said the same thing. We felt a sense of loss for our Mother but that jail time for Shawn would not serve any purpose for him or his family. Deb and I were in agreement about that.

Ultimately, the judge took our recommendations, as much as the law would allow. Shawn would pay fines and court costs, have a short suspension of his driving privileges, a probationary period, took a driver safety course and community service. We were asked what community service we'd like to have him do, and, after some discussion, Deb came up with having him volunteer at a school helping kids read. That was a great idea on her part. It seemed very appropriate, since that was one of Mom's favorite activities after she retired from the school. The court followed through with that recommendation. Apparently, Shawn was very good at it. We were glad that God worked that out for him too.

After the hearing was over, Shawn's wife, Amber, approached me.

"Thank you for being so kind," she sputtered through tear-drenched eyes. "You can't understand how much this means to our family and to Shawn." She gave me a huge hug.

As I teared up also, I said simply, "It was important to us that he be with his kids and with you. Removing him from your home does no one any good. He's a good man that made a bad mistake. He needs to hear that our family forgives him. He needs to go on with his life now and raise those kids."

Shawn was talking to his lawyer, and I slowly moved his way.

His eyes were bursting with tears and he could hardly speak.

"Thank you. Thank you. Thank you." He whispered those words so softly as we embraced that they were nearly inaudible, but they resounded in my mind as though he were using a bullhorn.

"Your wife needs you. Your kids need you. Count them as blessings every day." The words weren't mine. I wasn't even thinking about them. God's Holy Spirit was giving me those words and I couldn't stop.

"They love you and so do we." Wow, had I really just said that? It seemed so foreign to me. And yet, in my heart, I meant it. I knew

God was in charge, and I knew that his Son, Jesus Christ, would have said something similar to that. I was just saying and doing what I was commanded. I now understood the verse that came back to me, "Love your neighbor." Shawn and Amber and their family would work it all out. They were strong in their faith and God would protect them.

"Lord, put a hedge of protection around them. Guide them through the trying times as you have done with us. Show them Your love in ways they can't even imagine right now. Fill their measure to overflowing. Surround them with family and friends that will support them and give them strength. Thank You for showing me the way to love unequivocally, without conditions and in a way only You can empower us to love. In His Name, Amen."

I prayed hard on my way home and then sat back and enjoyed the ride. The sun had come out and most of the snow that had fallen was gone. I called Cheryl and Deb to let them know how things had gone. I was so glad this part was over. One more step that God had led us through and had blessed me also. It was right. It was all right. The blessings were still falling on me. Deb and I had decided to take the "high road" in all of this. I was so glad we did. God was showing His love for us and for Shawn's family. When we give blessings to others, they are returned many fold. God is good.

CHAPTER 25

"...honor your father and mother, and 'love your neighbor as yourself.'"

– Matthew 19:19 (NIV)

I don't know that I would call Shawn a friend—yet. I guess that depends upon which definition of friend one uses. My thoughts concerning friendship have been turned upside down since all of this happened. God has changed my heart and my perspective on who and what a friend, neighbor, or acquaintance is.

Dealing strictly Biblically, I guess everyone who becomes an acquaintance is automatically defined as a neighbor, as in, "love your neighbor as yourself." So, if we are to love a neighbor that strongly, would that person, also then be defined as a "friend"? How do we know for sure? Certainly I am waxing philosophical here, but it brings up a very good point. We are commanded in Luke 6 to love our enemies and pray for them so that our reward will be great in Heaven. I have never considered Shawn an enemy, quite the contrary. But, if we were commanded to love our enemies and pray for them, why then would we not pray for our acquaintances or our friends? Admittedly, I don't pray for my friends as much as I pray for my nuclear family. I don't pray for my church family as much as I should, either. Even after all these blessings, I am selfish. I don't pass them on enough.

I do pray for Shawn's family quite a bit. I have seen him a couple of times since that day in court. He is healing, slowly. My heart pours out to him every time we talk. We've talked on the telephone several times, especially around the Holidays. Recently, we had an invitation to go to their home, meet their children and have dinner with them. We had a phenomenal evening. We truly enjoyed our time of fellowship and God blessed both families, I believe. It was nice until we actually started talking about the events nearly three years earlier. Shawn is still devastated by it all. Deb and I have forgiven him, but he is still having trouble forgiving himself. He is so tenderhearted that he may never be completely over it. He is the epitome of a gentle giant.

As we move on from this time in our lives, there will forever be a link between our family and his. It is indisputable. We cannot separate the events from the bond it has created. We will be intertwined, irrevocably for the rest of our lives, and even perhaps, for the lives of the next generation as well. God works in miraculous ways. He often uses major life events to get our attention; to draw us to Him; to point out areas in which we need to improve or just to show His love for us. When I look back on all we, as a family, have been through, a few thoughts come flooding through.

- God is all-powerful. He is completely in charge of everything.

  - *"He said to me: 'It is done. I am the Alpha and the Omega, the Beginning and the End. To him who is thirsty I will give to drink without cost from the spring of the water of life. He who overcomes will inherit all this, and I will be his God and he will by my son.'" – Revelation 21:6-7 (NIV)*

- We must yield to His power and accept his grace, his peace and his mercy.

  - *"Be still and know that I am God. I will be exalted among the nations, I will be exalted in the earth." – Psalm 46:6 (NIV)*

  - *"From the fullness of his grace, we have all received one blessing after another." – John 1:16 (NIV)*

  - *"Peace I leave with you; my peace I give you. I do not give to you as the world gives. Do not let your hearts be troubled and do not be afraid." – John 14:27 (NIV)*

  - *"His mercy extends to those who fear him, from generation to generation." – Luke 1:50 (NIV)*

- He will give us the ability to handle all that comes our way if we allow him to be in control.

  - *"Trust in the Lord with all your heart and lean not on your own understanding; in all your ways submit to Him and He will make your paths straight." – Proverbs 3:5-6 (NIV)*

- We become better people, better Christians and better members of our society when we live, as He wants us to live.

  - *You are the light of the world. A town built on a hill cannot be hidden. Neither do people light a lamp and put it under a bowl. Instead they put it on its stand, and it gives light to everyone in the house. In the same way, let your light shine before others, that they may see your good deeds and glorify your Father in heaven." – Matthew 5:14-16 (NIV)*

- We must recognize that nothing we do that is worthwhile will ever be easy, but God grants us the ability to accomplish it if we are willing to allow Him to work through us.

  - *"But we have this treasure in jars of clay to show that this all-surpassing power is from God and not from us. We are hard pressed on every side, but not crushed; perplexed, but not in despair; persecuted, but not abandoned; struck down, but not destroyed…All this is for your benefit, so that the grace that is reaching more and more people may cause thanksgiving to overflow to the glory of God. Therefore we do not lose heart. Though outwardly we are wasting away, yet inwardly we are being renewed day by day… So we fix our eyes not on what is seen, but on what is unseen, since what is seen is temporary but what is unseen is eternal." – 2 Corinthians 4: 7-9,15-16 & 18 (NIV)*

- If we are thankful for everything that happens to us—good or bad—God will bless us in ways we can never imagine.

  - *"…always giving thanks to God the Father for everything, in the name of our Lord Jesus Christ" – Ephesians 5:20 (NIV)*

My hope for you is that these pages have inspired, challenged and encouraged you. What we do with our lives and how others perceive us is almost entirely based on the attitudes we possess. If we are God-inspired, we will show a beacon of light to all with whom we come into contact. *"They will know we are Christians by our love."* This kind of love comes only from our Heavenly Father and from His Precious Son, Jesus Christ through the indwelling of the Holy Spirit. I hope for you this same knowledge and experience in times of trial and tribulation. Whether it might be work-related, financial or something as deep as the loss of a loved one. Please pray and give thanks for each "difficult" situation, then stand back and watch God bless you in ways that you cannot imagine. He promised to do that; all you have to do is claim it. May God's blessings pour down on you forever, and ever, Amen.

Oh and by the way, Shawn and God are friends of mine.

ADDENDA

I have included some of the supplementary materials in these Addenda. Contained herein are the victim statements that were read in the courtroom, Deb's "Memories of Mom" that she had read at the funeral, and the memoriam that Rachel and Arielle read at the funeral.

VICTIM IMPACT STATEMENT
DEBRA S. (HORD) HOLLINGER
DAUGHTER OF MARILYN ANN HORD

On the evening of March 24, 2011, I received a phone call from my brother indicating that our mother had been involved in a head-on crash on US Route 224 outside Attica, Ohio, and had been taken by life-flight to St. Vincent's Mercy Medical Center in Toledo, Ohio. She passed away as a result of her injuries just after 12:00 a.m. on March 31.

The loss of my mother has impacted my family and me greatly. It has been most difficult for our granddaughter, Noel, now age 3, who was very close to her great-grandmother. The weekend prior to the crash, Mom had kept Noel from Thursday-Sunday—something she did almost every month. They both looked forward to those times together, which will never be again. Noel understands, in her own way, that Great-grandma lives with Jesus now, but she still asks when she will be able to go stay with Great-grandma and Jesus.

Our daughter Rachel, a single mother, was also very close to her Grandma. They talked at least once a week, if not more often, and Rachel went to my mother for guidance on life and raising her daughter. On nearly a daily basis, she has to deal with the questions from Noel and comments Noel makes about Great-grandma. It is very rough on her. My husband Michael has also felt the loss and commented quite often about what a good mother-in-law she was.

When it comes to the impact this loss had had on me, it is profound. I used to call Mom on my way to and/or home from work. The first week she was gone and I was back at work, I caught myself trying to call her several times. Easter came and went—a holiday she loved and loved to make special for all of us. There will be no more holiday celebrations with her. Noel's birthday was just a week after her death. She will never be at another birthday celebration for any of us. While our days are not guaranteed to us, she was still so vibrant and enjoyed life so much that I feel she had a lot to live for and would have been around a long time.

This world has lost a mother, mother-in-law, grandmother, great-grandmother, sister, friend, companion, businesswoman, and servant of God. We only have memories of days gone by and hope for the future of eternity together. It is not ours to question why, and with the severity of her injuries, Mom would never have been the same. I don't wish her back with the disabilities she probably would have had, but I miss her terribly. No amount of money or no time served by Mr. _____ will bring her back. I do not want to see Mr. _____'s family torn apart by a long jail sentence or a large dollar amount of fines. There is no price that can be put on a human life, which was taken away so tragically.

Victim Impact Statement
Randy L. Hord, Son

Thank you for this chance to address the court.

On March 24, 2011, my mother, Marilyn Hord was involved in a car crash that eventually took her life. She passed away on March 31, 2011 after a week of Intensive Care at Toledo St. Vincent's Hospital.

Mom was a vibrant 79 year-old woman who loved gardening, volunteering at the school to help underprivileged kids learn to read and fulfilling her responsibilities as township clerk, which helped to keep her mind alert. She had many friends with whom she loved to spend time chatting, shopping or just going out to eat. She loved her granddaughters and spent a great deal of time doting over her great-granddaughter, Noel. She was a great lady.

This car wreck forever changed our lives and Mr. _____'s, as well.

My heart, and that of our family, goes out to Mr. _____ and his family. He, by all accounts, is a good, hard-working man trying the best he can to support his family. Undoubtedly, if he had it to do again, things would be much different.

As a teacher, I come into contact daily with students who live with only one parent, or, at times with students who live with neither biological parent. I see the devastating effect this has on those students and their self-esteem. It becomes a struggle for them, especially in their elementary years, to maximize their potential. This man has a lovely family, and a loving wife that cares very deeply for him and supports him. His children need him to be around, to spend time with them, to love them and to nurture them in a way only a father can. God intended children to be raised by a mother and a father. Removing him from this family for a length of time would create scars on these youngsters that might never heal.

As my family and I discussed what we would like to see happen to Mr. _____ relative to this charge, many ideas were put forth. But ultimately, the Godly thing that kept rising up, that kept burning on our consciences, was that his family, these kids, and his wonderful, loving wife need him. He is not a bad person. He is a person that made a bad mistake. For this reason, your honor, as the eldest child of Marilyn Hord, I am asking for leniency in your ruling for punishment for Mr. _____. We are not looking for vengeance, as it is not ours to take. Only God has the right to take vengeance on anyone. We are not looking for pity, as it is not what Mom would want us to do. She never sought pity through many of her life trials. We are not looking for any sort of extreme punishment because this man, and his family have suffered enough through the last four and a half months since the crash.

Please understand, we miss our mother dearly, but no amount of jail time, no amount of money, no vengeance will bring her back. She's in a better place than this world has to offer. The love she taught us to show to our family and to each other, we wish to extend to Mr. _____ and his family in the same way that Jesus showed His love for us.

Thank you, your honor, for this opportunity to address this court and to present our wishes to you.

Deb's Memoriam

Praise God from whom all blessings flow
Praise Him above all creatures here below
Praise Him above ye Heavenly Host
Praise Father, Son, and Holy Ghost

For those of us raised in the Church these words are very familiar. These are also the last words we shared before we left Mom's bedside just after she crossed over into Paradise. We had just completed the last leg of our "Journey of Praise" as Randy calls it, and it felt only fitting to me to lead those of us in that room in this familiar praise song. Mom had just gone home and was in the arms of Jesus with Daddy and Murray looking on and waiting their turns to hold her and welcome her.

Praise was always important to Mom whether it was directed to the God she loved, or to one of us for a job well done.

Mom was a patient teacher. One of my earliest memories of her was teaching me to sew. Before I started school she taught me the pride, which goes with a job well done. I made the dress I wore for my very first day of school, with her loving hands showing me what to do. When I was "finishing the seams" (putting stitching along the edge to keep them from raveling) she said her grandma had taught her that you have to make it look as nice on the inside as it does on the outside. I never forgot that statement, and to this day, feel like whatever I sew has to be perfect. I wish I could remember how many years she stayed up all night with me so I could finish my 4-H sewing projects the night before the judging-*probably all 11 years!* She quietly told me, when a mistake was made, "You know what you need to do," and handed me the seam ripper. No mater what life lesson she was teaching me, it was usually seasoned with a good deal of patience because I usually just didn't get it the first time through!

Mom always had a sense of adventure. Many Sundays we would load up in the car to go for a drive. Whether they had a plan or not, we never knew but Mom and Dad would drive us to see something new. The day's end usually resulted in a stop at McDonald's in Mansfield-the closest one at the time-for a burger, fries and shake. We ventured to new places on family vacations, camping first in a station wagon and progressing through the succession of a tent and pop-up camper and fifth-wheel, which allowed them to have even more adventures in their "empty nest" years.

One of my most vivid memories was Mom telling us, "If you are too sick to go to church, you are too sick to do anything else." That principle was very strictly adhered to-especially for those aforementioned Sunday drives. Church was always a top priority, and when the doors were open, The Hord family was there! There are memories of Easter Sunrise Services and Breakfasts, youth group trips when they were youth leaders, and first the overall underlying current that God and Church were #1 with her. She had a rock-solid faith that was unshakeable. I caught her many times reading her Bible and praying for everyone she could think of. In recent years, she would make statements like, "I read this in my devotions today…" or "I was just reading in the Bible the other day…" I take great joy and peace in knowing that many years ago, she asked the Lord into her heart and lived a quiet faith her entire life.

Mom was a wonderful wife, loving mom, fantastic grandma, and a super great-grandma. Just the weekend before her tragic accident she had our granddaughter, Noel, for the weekend, as she did about once a month. They thoroughly enjoyed each other's company and as soon as Mom returned Noel to us, she was asking when she could have her again.

Mom was private with her personal life, but welcoming and open to others and their needs. She was compassionate, most of the time, but I remember her coming after us with the yardstick more than once! She was beautiful, both inside and out, and prided herself in looking nice when she left the house. She was energetic and vibrant. She was a woman who I was proud to call Mom and would hope that her influence in my life would allow the light of Jesus to shine through to others and her faith will be an inspiration to me as I take the rest of my journey through life.

She was loved dearly and will be sorely missed by all who knew her. I could go on and on with memories but I won't take the time to do that. God bless you for the part you played in her life, and keep us in your prayers in the days and weeks to come.

Grandma's ABC's

Arielle and Rachel

- A – A shopping trip and lunch for our birthdays
- B – Body Powder with the Powder Puff after baths at Grandma's house
- C – Chicken noodle soup and cereal with baby spoons-until we were teenagers
- D – Discovering new technology...the DVD player and watching movies with Murray to pass the afternoon
- E – Enormous bows at Christmas just to be goofy
- F – Flyswatters-and Grandma coming after us with them

G – Giving us the "Grandma Look" when we did something she didn't agree with

H – Hugs and Cuddles after baths

I – Idiot mittens made with love

J – Jumping on the furniture was a big no-no at Grandma's house

K – King's Best Friend

L – Leon's Partner in Crime

M – Making dish cloths on the knitting machine

N – Naked babies after bath and running down the hall to show off

O – Overnight sleepovers on the flip chairs

P – Pictures taken in matching, Grandma-made outfits

Q – Queen Bee—it's Grandma's way or get stung!

R – Reading bedtime stories

S – Stockings made with care and filled with love

T – Traveling while camping and site-seeing

U – Understanding

V – Van trips in the conversion van-everyone scrunched to go see the Christmas lights

W – World Book Cyclo-Teacher for hours of fun and Walkie Talkies with each other-one in the bedroom and one in the shop, sometimes both in the shop!

X – Xtra love and kisses always cured the boo-boos

Y – Young at Heart—a Great-Grandma able to care for a hyper-active toddler for a weekend

Z – Zoo trips on Mother's Day with the whole family

CPSIA information can be obtained
at www.ICGtesting.com
Printed in the USA
FFHW02n0219101018
48756412-52835FF